Social Currents:

Understanding Change in Modern Societies

Social Currents: Understanding Change in Modern Societies

Published By: Wissira Research Lab LLC

Imprint Name: Wissira Press

US Office: Carmel, United States- 46074

India Office: KDP, RNE, India-201017

Email: editor@wissira.us, Website: https://books.wissira.us

Mobile: +91 7535 916 555

Dr. Sanat Kumar Singha

ISBN - 978-93-7559-480-2

Maharaja Agrasen Himalayan Garhwal University,

Address: Uttarakhand, India

Edition: 2026

Printed In: India

Maharaja Agrasen Himalayan Garhwal University,

Address: Uttarakhand, India

Social Currents:

Understanding Change in Modern Societies

2026

Author:

Dr. Sanat Kumar Singha

Published By

Wissira Research Lab

ISBN 978-93-7559-480-2

9 789375 594802

Preface

In an era marked by rapid technological advancements, globalization, and shifting social dynamics, understanding the forces driving change in modern societies is more critical than ever. *Social Currents: Understanding Change in Modern Societies* aims to provide a comprehensive exploration of how societies evolve, adapt, and respond to the myriad challenges and opportunities that define our globalized world.

The study of social change is both fascinating and complex, as it involves examining multiple facets of human experience-from cultural transformations and shifting identities to the economic, political, and technological forces that shape social structures. The aim of this book is not just to chart the history of these changes, but to understand their implications for individuals, communities, and nations across the globe. By delving into topics like globalization, migration, inequality, social justice, and the future of social resilience, this book presents a holistic view of the ongoing transformations in the way we live, work, and relate to one another.

Each chapter of *Social Currents* focuses on a different aspect of social change, offering both theoretical insights and practical applications. From the foundational concepts of social change in Chapter 1 to the examination of technology's influence on social dynamics in Chapter 4, and the deep dive into inequality and social justice in Chapter 8, the book provides readers with an in-depth understanding of the forces that continue to shape societies worldwide. It also addresses the future trajectories of social change, urging us to consider how we can build inclusive, adaptive, and resilient communities in the face of ongoing challenges.

This book is intended for students, researchers, and anyone with a keen interest in understanding the complexities of modern society. It combines academic rigor with real-world examples and case studies to make the subject matter accessible and relevant. Whether you're studying sociology, economics, political science, or simply curious about the shifting landscape of our global community, *Social Currents* offers valuable insights into the forces that are reshaping our world.

We hope that this work inspires further inquiry and discussion about the ways in which we can collectively navigate the future, fostering social change that is equitable, sustainable, and responsive to the needs of all members of society. As we continue to confront the challenges of the 21st century, it is crucial to understand not just where we are headed, but how we can actively shape the direction of our social future.

Author:

Dr. Sanat Kumar Singha

Overview of the Book

Social Currents: Understanding Change in Modern Societies offers an insightful examination of the complex, multifaceted processes that shape social structures, cultural norms, economic systems, and political landscapes in the 21st century. In an age marked by rapid technological advancements, global interconnectedness, and shifting socio-political paradigms, this book provides a comprehensive framework for understanding how modern societies evolve and respond to the challenges of an increasingly complex world.

The book is organized into nine chapters, each focusing on a specific dimension of social change. These chapters draw upon both historical analysis and contemporary case studies, offering a balanced perspective that highlights the forces driving social transformation and the ways in which societies adapt, resist, or embrace change.

Chapter 1: Society in Motion – Foundations of Social Change

The first chapter introduces the concept of social change, exploring its definition, nature, and the various factors that drive it. It examines both gradual and abrupt shifts in societal structures, values, and behaviours, offering insights into the fundamental processes that lead to transformation in social systems.

Chapter 2: Culture, Identity, and the Transformation of Social Norms

This chapter focuses on the role of culture in social change, exploring how traditions, values, and norms evolve over time. It examines the fluidity of cultural identities and how societal values related to gender, ethnicity, and religion are redefined as global and local influences converge.

Chapter 3: Economic Transitions and the Reshaping of Social Life

Economic systems are a cornerstone of social life, and Chapter 3 delves into the changes that have reshaped economies over time. From industrialization to the rise of the digital economy, this chapter explores how economic shifts influence class structures, labour markets, and patterns of consumption.

Chapter 4: Technology, Media, and the Digital Social Order

The fourth chapter examines the powerful role of technology and media in shaping modern societies. It explores how digital advancements, social media, and the internet have transformed communication, interaction, and access to information.

Chapter 5: Politics, Power, and Social Movements in a Changing World

Chapter 5 delves into the interplay between political power and social movements, emphasizing how movements for social justice and political change are often catalysed by underlying societal shifts.

Chapter 6: Family, Education, and Social Institutions in Transition

This chapter addresses the transformation of key social institutions, particularly the family and education system. It examines how changing gender roles, marriage patterns, and family structures reflect broader social trends.

Chapter 7: Globalization, Migration, and Cross-Cultural Interactions

Globalization and migration are central themes in modern social change. This chapter explores how the movement of people, ideas, and goods across borders creates both opportunities for cultural exchange and tensions related to identity and belonging.

Chapter 8: Inequality, Social Justice, and Emerging Divides

The eighth chapter explores the persistent issue of inequality in contemporary societies. It highlights the economic, racial, and gender divides that persist despite advancements in many areas.

Chapter 9: The Future of Social Change – Continuity, Adaptation, and Resilience

The final chapter looks forward, considering the future trajectories of social change. It explores themes of resilience, adaptation, and sustainability, emphasizing how societies can learn to navigate and adapt to the rapid changes unfolding around them.

Table of Contents

1

Society in Motion – Foundations of Social Change

1.1 Understanding Society as a Dynamic System

Society is not a fixed or static entity; it is a living system shaped by continuous interactions among individuals, groups, and institutions. Social relationships, norms, and structures evolve as people respond to changing circumstances such as population growth, technological innovation, and environmental conditions.

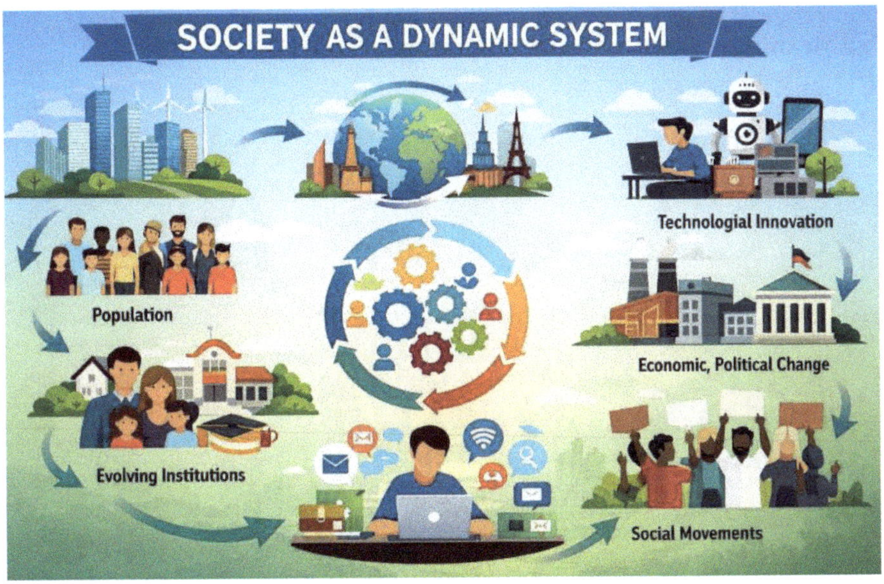

Society is a constantly evolving system, not a rigid or unchanging entity. It is shaped by the ongoing interactions between individuals, communities, and institutions. These interactions are influenced by various factors, including technological advancements, demographic changes, and shifts in cultural or environmental conditions.

The dynamic nature of society allows for a continuous process of adaptation. For instance, societal norms and values may change in response to shifts in economic or political landscapes, technological innovations, or movements for social justice. These changes can result in the transformation of institutions such as the family, education systems, or governments, which evolve to meet new needs or address emerging challenges.

Understanding society as a dynamic system enables sociologists to explore how and why traditions and practices evolve over time. For example, in response to globalization, cultural exchanges have led to a blending of practices from different societies, altering traditional ways of life. Similarly, the rise of the digital age has transformed how people communicate, work, and access information, thereby reshaping social structures and relationships.

1.2 Meaning and Nature of Social Change

Social change refers to significant alterations in social behaviour, cultural values, and institutional arrangements across time. These changes may be gradual, such as shifts in family roles, or rapid, such as political revolutions.

Social change refers to the transformation or significant modifications in social behaviours, cultural values, and institutional structures over time. These changes can occur at various paces-gradual changes, such as evolving family roles or the shift in gender norms, often occur over decades or generations. On the other hand, rapid social changes, such as political revolutions or technological breakthroughs, can happen in a matter of years or even months, profoundly impacting the social fabric.

The nature of social change is deeply intertwined with how individuals and groups think, work, communicate, and organize themselves within a society. It affects everyday life by influencing everything from social relationships to work structures. For example, the rise of the digital age has fundamentally changed communication patterns, with social media replacing traditional forms of interaction and affecting how people share information and organize social movements.

Social change is also inevitable, as societies are always evolving in response to new influences such as technological advancements, economic pressures, or shifts in political ideologies. However, the process of change is not uniform; it is uneven across different segments of society. The impact of social change varies based on factors such as power dynamics, access to resources, and the prevailing social or political climate. For instance, social changes that benefit the economically privileged may not have the same positive impact on marginalized communities, highlighting the unequal distribution of benefits that may result from these shifts.

1.3 Factors Driving Social Change

Multiple forces contribute to social change, including technological advancements, economic development, population dynamics, and ideological movements. Education and communication play a critical role

in spreading new ideas, while conflicts and crises often accelerate transformation.

Social change is influenced by a wide range of factors that shape and transform societies over time. These factors are often interconnected, creating complex pathways through which change occurs. Below are some of the key drivers of social change:

Technological Advancements
One of the most powerful forces behind social change is technological innovation. New technologies can revolutionize how people work, communicate, and interact with the environment. For instance, the invention of the internet and smartphones has drastically altered communication, work environments, and social interactions globally. Social media platforms, for example, have changed how individuals engage with one another, spread information, and mobilize for social causes, contributing to the rise of movements such as the Arab Spring or #MeToo.

2. Economic Development
Economic factors are another critical driver of social change. Economic growth can lead to changes in class structures, wealth distribution, and access to resources. The industrial revolution, for instance, radically transformed societies by shifting economies from agriculture to manufacturing, creating urbanization, and altering the traditional family structure. In modern times, the rise of the digital economy and the gig economy is reshaping employment patterns, work culture, and economic inequalities.

3. Population Dynamics
Changes in population size, density, migration, and demographics also play a significant role in shaping society. Population growth can lead to urbanization, strain on resources, and changes in social structures, such as family dynamics and social services. For example, rapid urbanization in developing countries has led to the expansion of megacities and shifts in social behaviour, employment opportunities, and access to public services.

Migration patterns also influence cultural exchange, challenging existing social norms and promoting diversity.

4. Ideological Movements

Social and political ideologies, such as feminism, civil rights, or environmentalism, drive societal change by advocating for shifts in values, rights, and norms. These movements often challenge the status quo and push for reforms that impact laws, policies, and social structures. The feminist movement, for example, has been instrumental in challenging gender roles and advocating for women's rights, leading to legislative changes such as equal pay laws and reproductive rights.

5. Education and Communication

Education and communication are powerful tools in spreading new ideas and fostering social change. The expansion of education systems, particularly in the modern era, has empowered individuals with knowledge and critical thinking skills, which can lead to a more informed and active citizenry. Additionally, advancements in communication technology, such as television, radio, and the internet, have enabled the rapid dissemination of new ideas, ideologies, and movements across global communities.

6. Conflicts and Crises

Conflicts, wars, and crises, whether economic, environmental, or political, often accelerate social change. These events can disrupt the established order, forcing societies to rethink their values, systems, and structures. For instance, World War II led to significant changes in global power structures, the establishment of the United Nations, and the creation of new international norms. Similarly, environmental crises such as climate change are driving global movements toward sustainability and reshaping policies and practices regarding resource use.

Interactions Among These Factors

It is important to note that these factors do not operate in isolation. Instead, they interact and often reinforce one another. For example, technological advancements may drive economic growth, which in turn affects population dynamics and social structures. Similarly, ideological movements can gain momentum through the support of new communication technologies or economic systems. As a result, social change is rarely linear; it is shaped by a complex interplay of these multiple factors.

Perspective	Key Focus	Example
Functionalist Perspective	Progress and Adaptation	Technological advances leading to changes in work environments, such as automation transforming the labour market and educational systems adapting to new skill demands.
Conflict Perspective	Inequality and Power Struggles	The civil rights movement in the U.S. challenging racial inequality and segregation, or labour movements advocating for workers' rights.
Cultural and Ideological Perspective	Shifting Values and Beliefs	The feminist movement changing societal views on gender roles and advocating for women's rights, including legal changes related to gender equality.
Social Constructionist Perspective	The Role of Human Agency	The LGBTQ+ rights movement challenging traditional understandings of sexuality and gender, leading to changes in policies, marriage equality, and gender identity recognition.
Ecological Perspective	Environmental and Global Factors	Global movements for sustainability, renewable energy, and environmental justice due to increasing concerns about climate change.

Multiple Choice Questions (MCQs)

1. Which of the following best describes social change?

a) A sudden and temporary shift in societal norms.
b) A significant alteration in social behaviour, cultural values, and institutional arrangements over time.
c) The preservation of societal norms without any transformation.
d) A process that is always resisted by society.

Answer: b) A significant alteration in social behaviour, cultural values, and institutional arrangements over time.

2. According to the functionalist perspective, social change is seen as:

a) A process driven primarily by conflict and power struggles.
b) A process of gradual adaptation necessary to maintain social stability and equilibrium.
c) A disruption that always leads to societal collapse.
d) A result of sudden shifts in ideological movements.

Answer: b) A process of gradual adaptation necessary to maintain social stability and equilibrium.

3. Which factor is considered a major driver of social change according to the conflict perspective?

a) Technological innovation.
b) Power struggles and inequalities between groups.
c) Education and communication systems.
d) Government reforms and policies.

Answer: b) Power struggles and inequalities between groups.

4. What role does education play in social change?

a) It has no significant role in driving social change.
b) It is a tool for maintaining the status quo by reinforcing traditional values.

c) It spreads new ideas and helps individuals adapt to changing societal norms.
d) It exclusively focuses on imparting vocational skills without influencing societal values.

Answer: c) It spreads new ideas and helps individuals adapt to changing societal norms.

5. Which of the following is an example of social change driven by ideological movements?

a) The rise of the internet leading to new ways of communication.
b) The feminist movement advocating for gender equality and influencing legal changes.
c) Economic development leading to urbanization.
d) Migration patterns causing demographic shifts in society.

Answer: b) The feminist movement advocating for gender equality and influencing legal changes.

Short Answer Questions

1. What is the definition of social change?
2. How does the functionalist perspective view social change?
3. What role do technological advancements play in social change?
4. Explain the conflict perspective on social change.
5. Why is education considered an important factor in driving social change?
6. Give an example of a social movement that has led to significant social change.

Long Answer Questions

1. Explain the concept of social change and discuss its various driving forces. How do factors like technology, economy, and population dynamics contribute to it?

2. Discuss the different theoretical perspectives on social change. How do functionalism, conflict theory, and social constructionism explain the process of social transformation? Provide examples for each.

3. Examine the role of conflicts and crises in accelerating social change. Discuss with examples of historical events where social crises led to significant transformations in society.

4. How do ideological movements drive social change? Provide an analysis of a specific ideological movement and explain its impact on societal values and structures.

5. Explore the tension between continuity and transformation in social change. Why do some aspects of society remain stable while others evolve? How do these tensions shape the course of social change?

6. Describe the interaction between various factors such as technology, economic development, and population dynamics in shaping the direction of social change. How do these factors work together to influence societal evolution?

2

Culture, Identity, and the Transformation of Social Norms

2.1 Culture as a Framework for Social Life

Culture provides the shared meanings, values, and practices that guide social behaviour. It influences how people communicate, celebrate, work, and interpret the world around them. As societies encounter new ideas and experiences, cultural patterns evolve, blending tradition with innovation while maintaining a sense of collective identity.

Culture forms the bedrock of social life, providing the underlying framework that shapes the way people interact, behave, and perceive the world. It encompasses shared values, customs, beliefs, and practices that give meaning to everyday experiences. From language to rituals, art to cuisine, culture influences almost every aspect of human existence. It helps define what is considered acceptable or taboo, providing a common ground for individuals to relate to each other and society at large.

Cultural norms dictate not only how people communicate but also how they celebrate milestones, handle conflict, and work together. For instance, while individualism may be emphasized in Western cultures, collective group identity and interdependence often take precedence in Eastern societies. These cultural differences shape social interactions, impacting everything from business negotiations to familial relationships.

As societies face new challenges and adopt different influences-whether through technology, migration, or globalization-cultural patterns evolve. New ideas are often blended with traditional practices, leading to a dynamic cultural landscape. Yet, amidst these changes, the core aspects of culture often remain steadfast, offering individuals a sense of belonging and continuity. Culture, therefore, serves as a stabilizing force, preserving identity while simultaneously adapting to the evolving world around it.

2.2 Changing Social Norms and Values

Social norms are informal rules that regulate behaviour within a society. Over time, norms related to gender roles, family structures, and authority have undergone significant change. These shifts often reflect broader changes in education, economic participation, and social awareness, leading to greater questioning of previously unquestioned practices.

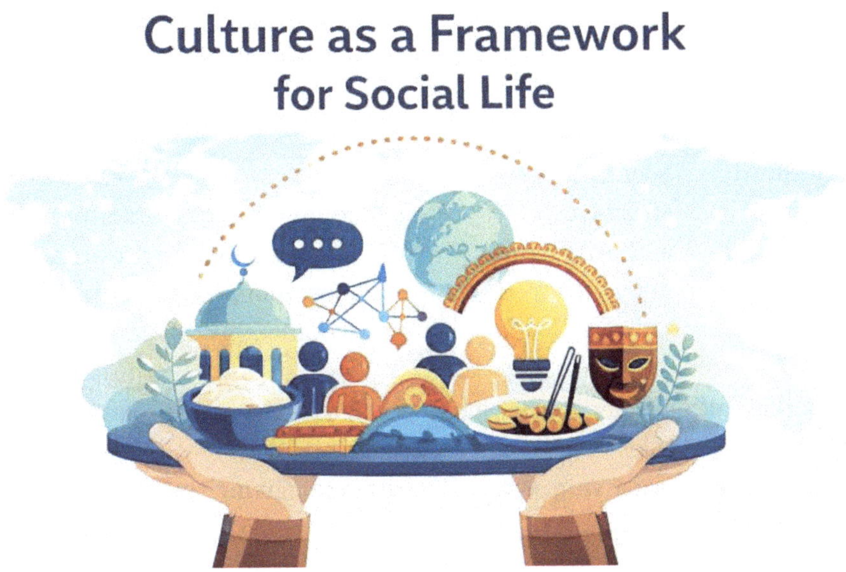

Social norms are unwritten guidelines that dictate how people should behave in various situations. These norms shape interactions, define acceptable behaviour, and foster a sense of order within a community. Over time, however, these norms can evolve, often reflecting deeper shifts in a society's values, priorities, and understanding of justice and equality. Changes in norms are not only a response to societal transformation but often act as a driving force for it.

Aspect	Traditional Norms	Modern Changes	Drivers of Change
Gender Roles	Men as primary breadwinners, women as caregivers	Increased women's workforce participation, shared household duties	Education, activism, gender equality movements
Family Structures	Nuclear family with two parents and children	Diverse family structures (e.g., single-parent, same-sex, multigenerational)	Changing societal attitudes, LGBTQ+ rights, economic challenges
Authority	Hierarchical structures, authority figures not questioned	Increased questioning of authority, demand for transparency and accountability	Access to information, rise of social media, generational shifts
Workplace Roles	Gender-specific job roles (e.g., men in leadership, women in support roles)	Women in leadership roles, men in caregiving roles	Education, economic necessity, breaking down of gender stereotypes
Marriage	Heteronormative, often arranged marriages	Acceptance of diverse sexual orientations, more autonomy in marriage choices	LGBTQ+ rights movements, changing cultural perceptions

One of the most noticeable areas where social norms have changed is in gender roles. Traditionally, many societies prescribed rigid roles for men and women, with women often relegated to domestic duties and men expected to be the primary breadwinners. In recent decades, however, these roles have become increasingly flexible. Women's participation in the workforce has grown, with many breaking barriers in fields once considered male-dominated, such as engineering, politics, and business. Likewise, men are more involved in household chores and child-rearing, reflecting a shift toward gender equality. This change is driven by various factors, including education, activism, and greater societal awareness of the need for gender equity.Family structures have also undergone significant transformations. In the past, the nuclear family-composed of two parents and their children-was seen as the dominant family model. Today, there is greater acceptance of diverse family arrangements, such as single-parent families, same-sex couples raising children, and multi-generational households. These changes are influenced by shifts in social attitudes, such as growing acceptance of LGBTQ+ rights and changing economic conditions, where financial challenges sometimes require families to adapt in ways that challenge traditional norms.

Another area where social norms have shifted is in authority structures. Historically, many societies placed great emphasis on hierarchy, where authority figures, such as elders, teachers, and religious leaders, were rarely questioned. Today, with the advent of greater access to information and the rise of social media, questioning authority has become more common. Younger generations, in particular, are more likely to challenge established norms and demand transparency and accountability from leaders in politics, business, and other sectors.

These changes in social norms are deeply interconnected with broader societal shifts. Economic participation, such as women entering the workforce, educational advancements, and increased global communication, all play roles in challenging traditional practices. Social awareness, fuelled by movements advocating for gender equality, LGBTQ+ rights, and racial justice, has led to questioning practices that were once unquestioned.

2.3 Identity Formation in Modern Societies

Identity is shaped by multiple social influences, including culture, class, gender, religion, and nationality. In modern societies, individuals increasingly negotiate their identities in flexible and complex ways. Exposure to diverse perspectives through migration, media, and education allows people to redefine who they are and how they relate to others.

Identity is a multifaceted construct shaped by various social influences, including culture, class, gender, religion, and nationality. These elements contribute to the way individuals perceive themselves and how they are perceived by others. In modern societies, identity formation has become increasingly complex and fluid, as people no longer feel confined to fixed categories or traditional labels. Instead, they engage in a process of continuous negotiation and redefinition of who they are, influenced by both internal and external factors.

One of the key influences on identity is **culture**, which provides the shared values, beliefs, and practices that inform an individual's worldview. Cultural backgrounds shape language, behaviour, and norms, offering a sense of belonging and continuity. However, as societies become more globalized, individuals are exposed to a variety of cultural perspectives, allowing them to blend elements of different cultures into their identity. This creates opportunities for hybrid identities that reflect diverse influences, particularly in urban centres where multiculturalism is more prominent.

Class also plays a significant role in identity formation. Economic status and social class can influence access to resources, opportunities, and networks, which in turn shape an individual's experiences and worldview. However, in modern societies, class mobility has become more attainable due to changes in education, technology, and labour markets. As a result, individuals from different socio-economic backgrounds may increasingly identify with values or social circles that transcend traditional class divisions.

Gender and **sexuality** are increasingly seen as fluid, rather than fixed. Traditional binary understandings of gender are being challenged by a growing recognition of gender diversity. Many individuals now navigate their gender identities in more flexible ways, allowing them to define themselves outside of rigid societal norms. Similarly, changing attitudes toward sexuality have led to a more inclusive understanding of diverse sexual orientations, enabling people to embrace identities that reflect their personal experiences and self-understanding.

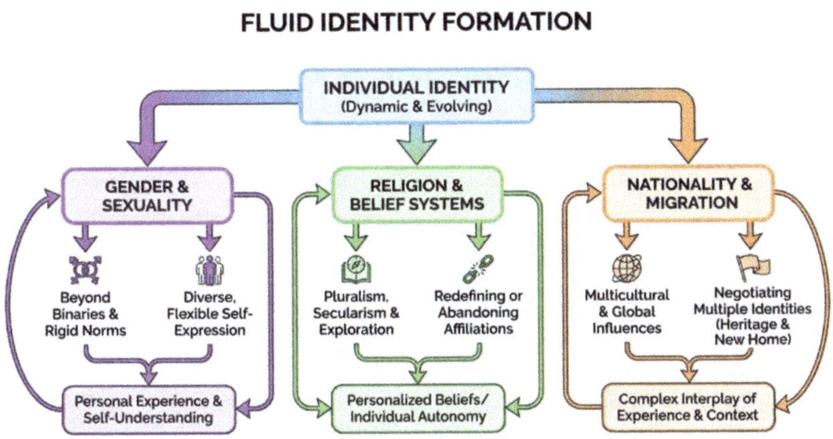

Religion remains an important factor in identity formation, but modern societies see increasing religious pluralism and secularism. People now have greater freedom to explore, redefine, or even abandon religious affiliations. In some cases, individuals may draw on elements from multiple religious traditions, integrating them into a personalized belief system, or they may adopt secular worldviews that prioritize individual autonomy over religious doctrine.

Nationality also influences identity, particularly in multicultural or immigrant societies. Migration and the global exchange of ideas have created opportunities for people to explore multiple national identities. People who migrate may negotiate their identity by balancing their heritage with the culture of their new home, often navigating the tension between the two.

National identity is no longer fixed in the way it once was; it is increasingly shaped by the complex interplay of personal experience and global influences.

2.4 Cultural Diversity and Social Adaptation

Cultural diversity has become a defining feature of contemporary societies. Interaction among different cultural groups encourages exchange, creativity, and mutual learning but can also create tensions.

Cultural diversity refers to the presence of various cultural groups within a society, each contributing unique values, practices, and worldviews. In contemporary societies, cultural diversity has become a defining feature, particularly in urban areas and in societies that experience high rates of migration and globalization. Interaction among these diverse groups presents both opportunities and challenges for social cohesion and integration.

On the positive side, cultural diversity promotes **exchange**, **creativity**, and **mutual learning**. When people from different cultural backgrounds come together, they bring a wealth of knowledge, traditions, and perspectives that can enrich social experiences. For instance, in multicultural cities like New York, London, or Toronto, residents have the opportunity to learn about and engage with different cuisines, festivals, music, and languages. This exchange not only broadens individuals' horizons but also sparks innovation by combining diverse ideas and problem-solving approaches. In businesses, cultural diversity can drive creativity, as teams made up of individuals from varied backgrounds often approach challenges from different angles, leading to more innovative solutions.

However, cultural diversity can also **create tensions**. Differences in values, customs, and social norms can lead to misunderstandings or conflicts between groups. For example, cultural clashes may arise when different groups have contrasting views on issues such as gender roles, religion, or authority. These tensions can sometimes lead to feelings of alienation, discrimination, or exclusion. In extreme cases, they can even foster divisiveness within a society, where certain groups may feel marginalized or underrepresented.

Successful **social adaptation** to cultural diversity requires careful management of these tensions. One key element in this process is **dialogue**. Open and respectful communication between cultural groups allows individuals to share their perspectives and understand each other's values and experiences. Dialogue helps to break down stereotypes and reduces fear of the unfamiliar, promoting mutual respect.

Another critical component of successful adaptation is **tolerance**. Tolerance does not mean complete agreement with all cultural practices, but rather the acceptance of differences and the recognition of each group's right to express their identity. In societies where tolerance is valued, people are more likely to respect the beliefs and practices of others, even if they do not personally identify with them.

Multiple Choice Questions (MCQs)

1. What is the primary influence of culture on social behaviour?

A) Culture primarily dictates how people dress

B) Culture provides shared values, beliefs, and practices that guide social behaviour

C) Culture only affects how people celebrate festivals

D) Culture influences only the language people speak

Answer: B) Culture provides shared values, beliefs, and practices that guide social behaviour

2. How has gender role perception changed in modern societies?

A) Gender roles have remained fixed and rigid across societies

B) Women's roles have expanded, and men are increasingly involved in caregiving and domestic duties

C) Men no longer participate in the workforce

D) Gender roles are now determined solely by economic class

Answer: B) Women's roles have expanded, and men are increasingly involved in caregiving and domestic duties

3. Which of the following is an example of social adaptation in a multicultural society?

A) Maintaining separate communities with little interaction

B) Ensuring the cultural practices of different groups are respected and included in public life

C) Forcing all groups to adopt a single cultural norm

D) Discouraging the expression of cultural differences

Answer: B) Ensuring the cultural practices of different groups are respected and included in public life

4. What is a key driver of identity formation in modern societies?

A) Adherence to fixed cultural traditions

B) Limited exposure to diverse perspectives

C) Increased interaction with different cultures, migration, media, and education

D) Strict adherence to national identity without external influence

Answer: C) Increased interaction with different cultures, migration, media, and education

5. What is the role of tolerance in managing cultural diversity?

A) It encourages people to abandon their own cultural beliefs

B) It ensures the full acceptance of all practices, regardless of their impact on society

C) It involves respecting differences while allowing each group to retain their unique identity

D) It forces individuals to conform to one dominant culture

Answer: C) It involves respecting differences while allowing each group to retain their unique identity

Short Answer Questions

1. What is cultural diversity, and why is it important in modern societies?
2. How have traditional gender roles evolved in contemporary societies?
3. Define social norms and explain their role in regulating behaviour within a society.
4. What factors contribute to the transformation of social norms over time?
5. How does exposure to different cultural perspectives influence identity formation?

Long Answer Questions

1. Discuss the impact of cultural diversity on creativity and innovation in modern societies. Provide examples where cultural exchange has led to significant social or technological advancements.
2. Explain how identity formation has become more flexible in modern societies. How do factors such as migration, media, and globalization influence how individuals define and negotiate their identities?
3. Examine the transformation of gender roles in modern societies. What are the driving factors behind the shift from traditional to more inclusive gender norms, and what challenges remain?
4. How do social norms related to family structures differ across cultures, and how have they evolved over time? Discuss the implications of these changes on family dynamics and societal values.
5. Analyse the role of education and media in shaping social norms and values in contemporary societies. How do these institutions influence the ways in which individuals adapt to societal changes?

3

Economic Transitions and the Reshaping of Social Life

3.1 Evolution of Economic Systems

Economic systems have evolved from agrarian economies to industrial and post-industrial forms. Each transition has altered patterns of production, employment, and social organization. Changes in economic structures influence lifestyles, settlement patterns, and the distribution of opportunities within society.

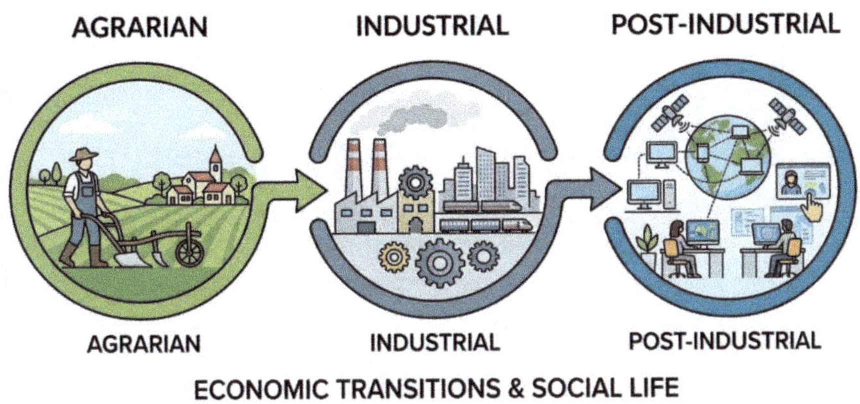

Economic systems have undergone significant transformations throughout history, evolving from primarily agrarian economies to industrial and, more recently, post-industrial or knowledge-based economies. Each phase of this evolution has brought about profound changes in how goods and services are produced, distributed, and consumed, shaping the broader social and cultural fabric of societies.

Agrarian Economies: In agrarian economies, the primary mode of production was agriculture. The majority of people were involved in farming or related activities, with land being the principal factor of production. Social organization in these economies was often hierarchical, with landowners at the top and labourers or peasants at the bottom. The distribution of wealth and resources was highly uneven, with limited opportunities for social mobility. Most societies were organized around rural settlements, and economic activity was closely tied to the seasons and agricultural cycles.

Industrial Economies: The Industrial Revolution, which began in the late 18th century, marked a dramatic shift in economic systems. The introduction of mechanized production and the rise of factories transformed the landscape of work, moving away from agriculture and cottage industries to large-scale manufacturing. This shift led to urbanization, as people moved from rural areas to cities in search of work. Industrial economies are characterized by mass production, wage labour, and the rise of capitalism. Employment opportunities expanded in factories, and new social classes, such as the working class and the industrial bourgeoisie, emerged. This transformation also led to significant changes in social structures, with greater emphasis on efficiency, innovation, and the division of labour.

Post-Industrial or Knowledge Economies : The transition to post-industrial or knowledge-based economies began in the mid-20th century, driven by advances in technology, information systems, and global communication. Unlike industrial economies, which were centred on manufacturing, post-industrial economies focus on the production and distribution of knowledge, services, and technology. In this phase, industries like information technology, healthcare, finance, and education dominate. Employment patterns shifted toward service-oriented jobs, and the demand for highly skilled labour increased, leading to a growing emphasis on education and specialization. This shift also led to changes in settlement patterns, with people increasingly living in urban areas, where they could access better job opportunities and infrastructure. Social organization became more complex, with new forms of inequality emerging based on access to education, technology, and knowledge.

3.2 Work, Occupations, and Changing Class Structures

Modern economies have transformed the nature of work, shifting from manual labour to service- and knowledge-based occupations. These changes have redefined social class structures and career mobility.

Modern economies have undergone a profound transformation in the nature of work, transitioning from predominantly manual labour to occupations focused on services and knowledge. These shifts have redefined traditional class structures and career mobility, significantly altering the way people approach their work, economic security, and social standing.

From Manual Labor to Service and Knowledge-Based Occupations : In earlier industrial economies, manual labour was the cornerstone of most jobs. Factory work, agriculture, and other physical labour-intensive industries dominated the workforce. However, as technological advancements progressed and the economy shifted towards industrialization and later to post-industrialism, there was a marked shift toward service-based and knowledge-based occupations. These new industries-ranging from healthcare and education to information technology, finance, and research-demanded a different skill set, such as specialized knowledge, technical expertise, and creative problem-solving abilities. In this context, work moved away from physical labour and towards intellectual, managerial, and service-oriented tasks.

Redefinition of Social Class Structures : The shift in the nature of work has had significant implications for social class structures. In traditional industrial societies, social class was largely determined by one's occupation-factory workers, labourers, and manual workers occupied the lower rungs, while professionals, managers, and business owners were at the top. However, as economies shifted toward services and knowledge sectors, the rigid boundaries between classes began to blur. The rise of highly skilled professions, such as engineers, scientists, and computer programmers, created new avenues for upward mobility, offering individuals from diverse backgrounds the potential to achieve greater wealth and status based on education and expertise rather than birthright or inheritance.

Yet, this shift has also introduced new complexities in class structures. The growing importance of education and specialized skills has created a divide between those who have access to advanced education and those who do not. The "knowledge gap" has, in some cases, replaced traditional class distinctions, with individuals who are highly skilled or educated occupying higher social strata, while those in low-skill, low-wage service jobs are often relegated to lower socio-economic classes.

Career Mobility and Job Insecurity : With the rise of service and knowledge-based economies, career mobility has become more fluid, but it has also introduced new challenges. On one hand, greater opportunities for education, training, and skills development have allowed people to move up the career ladder and shift industries. The tech boom, for instance, has created vast opportunities for people to enter high-paying, high-skill jobs, even in fields that did not exist a few decades ago. Additionally, globalization and digital technologies have facilitated the growth of remote work, providing workers with the ability to access job opportunities globally and enhancing their career mobility.

3.3 Consumption, Lifestyle, and Social Status

Economic growth influences patterns of consumption and lifestyle choices. Goods, services, and digital access often become markers of social status. Consumer culture shapes aspirations and social identities, linking economic capacity with perceptions of success and belonging in modern societies.

Economic growth has a profound influence on patterns of consumption and the choices individuals make regarding their lifestyles. As economies grow and new technologies emerge, consumption habits shift, and the ways in which people define success, identity, and social status also evolve. In modern societies, goods, services, and even access to digital technologies have become important markers of social status, shaping both aspirations and social identities.

Consumption as a Reflection of Economic Growth : As economies grow and prosper, there is often a corresponding increase in the availability and variety of goods and services. Economic growth leads to higher incomes and greater disposable wealth for many individuals, which in turn fuels consumer demand. In societies with higher levels of economic development, people have more access to diverse consumer goods, ranging from basic necessities to luxury items. This expansion of available products, particularly in sectors like electronics, fashion, and automobiles, allows individuals to express their preferences and aspirations through the things they consume. As people's purchasing power increases, their consumption habits tend to shift toward more non-essential, luxury, or status-enhancing goods.

Digital Access and Social Status : In the digital age, access to technology and the internet has become a major factor in determining social status. The ability to own and use the latest digital devices-smartphones, laptops, tablets, and high-speed internet access-has become a symbol of modernity, wealth, and success. This trend is especially pronounced in urban areas, where technology adoption is often faster, and digital literacy is higher. The ownership of high-end gadgets or the ability to access certain digital platforms (e.g., social media, streaming services, or online shopping) is now seen as a marker of one's social position. Furthermore, digital access enables individuals to participate in global consumer cultures, gain exposure to different lifestyles, and engage with digital communities, all of which shape their identities and aspirations.

Consumer Culture and Social Identity : Consumer culture plays a central role in shaping individual and collective identities in modern societies. What people buy and how they consume not only reflects their personal tastes but also signals their position within the broader social fabric. This phenomenon is especially evident in consumer-driven societies, were branding and advertising play significant roles in influencing consumer choices. The products individuals buy often become symbols of their social identities and aspirations. For instance, owning a luxury car or designer clothing can signal wealth, sophistication, and success, while the latest tech gadgets may reflect a person's connection to modernity and innovation.

3.4 Economic Inequality and Social Consequences

Unequal distribution of wealth and resources remains a major challenge in modern societies. Economic inequality affects access to education, healthcare, and political participation.

Economic inequality-the unequal distribution of wealth, income, and resources-is a persistent issue in modern societies, and its social consequences are profound and far-reaching. Despite periods of economic growth and development, disparities in wealth and access to resources have continued to grow in many parts of the world. These inequalities affect not only the economic well-being of individuals but also their access to critical services such as education, healthcare, and political participation. Understanding the social consequences of economic inequality is crucial for designing policies that foster fairness, social stability, and inclusive development.

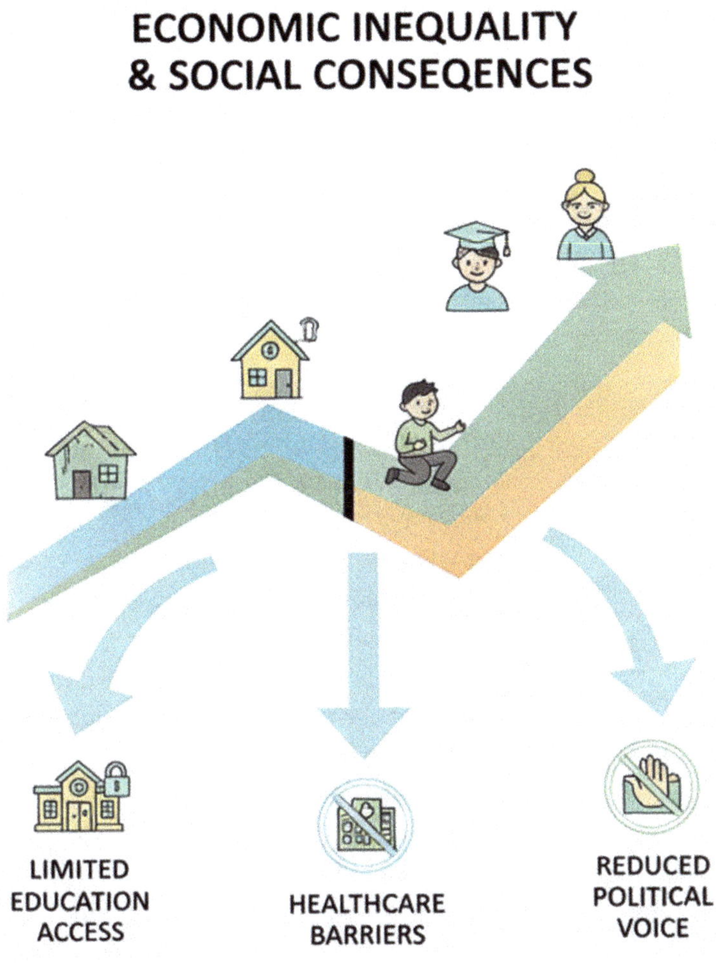

The Unequal Distribution of Wealth and Resources : Economic inequality arises from a variety of factors, including differences in education, employment opportunities, inheritance, and the ownership of assets. In many economies, wealth is concentrated in the hands of a small portion of the population, while the majority of individuals experience limited access to resources. This concentration of wealth often leads to economic structures that favour the wealthy, reinforcing existing power dynamics and social hierarchies. Those with significant financial resources have the ability to influence markets, politics, and even public policy, while the less fortunate are left with fewer opportunities to improve their living conditions.

This inequality is not only seen in income distribution but also in access to resources such as land, technology, and financial capital. Those who have access to these resources can invest in opportunities that generate wealth, while those who do not remain stuck in cycles of poverty and economic dependency. The result is a widening gap between the rich and the poor, leading to a stratified society where individuals' economic circumstances determine their opportunities and life chances.

Topic	Description
3.1 Evolution of Economic Systems	Economic systems have shifted from agrarian economies to industrial and post-industrial economies, changing patterns of production, employment, and social organization. These transitions affect lifestyles, settlement patterns, and opportunities.
3.2 Work, Occupations, and Changing Class Structures	Modern economies have transformed work from manual labour to service- and knowledge-based jobs, redefining social class structures and career mobility. This shift has brought new opportunities but also job insecurity and widened income disparities.
3.3 Consumption, Lifestyle, and Social Status	Economic growth influences consumption patterns and lifestyle choices. Goods, services, and digital access become markers of social status, shaping aspirations and social identities in modern societies.
3.4 Economic Inequality and Social Consequences	Economic inequality, through unequal distribution of wealth and resources, affects access to education, healthcare, and political participation. Understanding inequality's social consequences is crucial for policies promoting fairness and stability.

Impact on Education and Healthcare Access : One of the most significant consequences of economic inequality is its impact on access to education. In many societies, quality education is a key determinant of economic success, yet access to this education is often limited by an individual's economic status. Wealthier families are able to afford private schooling, tutoring, and other educational resources, while those from poorer backgrounds struggle to access even basic education. As a result, economic inequality perpetuates itself, with children from lower-income families often facing barriers to higher education and, consequently, to high-paying jobs.

Similarly, economic inequality affects access to healthcare. Wealthier individuals can afford private healthcare services, which often provide quicker and more comprehensive treatment. In contrast, those with limited financial resources are forced to rely on public health systems, which may be underfunded or overstretched. This disparity in healthcare access leads to unequal health outcomes, with poor individuals suffering from worse physical and mental health due to lack of access to quality care. Additionally, economic inequality often correlates with environmental factors that negatively impact health, such as living in areas with higher pollution or limited access to nutritious food.

Political Participation and Social Mobilization : Economic inequality also influences political participation. In societies where wealth is concentrated in the hands of a few, those with economic power are more likely to have access to political decision-makers and the ability to shape policy agendas. This leads to a political system where the interests of the wealthy are prioritized, while the concerns of poorer citizens are often neglected. Wealthier individuals are more likely to vote, donate to political campaigns, and have influence over policy decisions, which in turn perpetuates their social and economic advantages.

Multiple Choice Questions (MCQs)

1. Which of the following best describes the shift from agrarian economies to industrial economies?

a) Decrease in urbanization and migration

b) Shift from agricultural to manufacturing-based production

c) Focus on local trade and barter systems

d) Decline in technological advancements

Answer: b) Shift from agricultural to manufacturing-based production

2. What was one of the key social consequences of the Industrial Revolution?

a) Reduction in social hierarchies

b) Large-scale urbanization and the rise of cities

c) Decline in the importance of education

d) Reduction in global trade

Answer: b) Large-scale urbanization and the rise of cities

3. How have modern economies reshaped work and occupations?

a) Shift from service and knowledge-based jobs to manual labour

b) Increased reliance on physical labour and factory jobs

c) Rise of service- and knowledge-based occupations

d) Complete automation of all job sectors

Answer: c) Rise of service- and knowledge-based occupations

4. Which factor contributes to the widening of income disparities in modern economies?

a) Equal access to education and healthcare

b) Economic transitions leading to job insecurity

c) Decreased global competition

d) Increased government intervention in job markets

Answer: b) Economic transitions leading to job insecurity

5. How does economic inequality influence social mobility?

a) It creates more opportunities for upward mobility

b) It has no effect on social mobility

c) It hinders access to education, healthcare, and employment opportunities

d) It ensures equal opportunities for all citizens

Answer: c) It hinders access to education, healthcare, and employment opportunities

Short Answer Questions

1. What are the key features of an agrarian economy?
2. How did the Industrial Revolution affect patterns of production and employment?
3. What role does consumer culture play in shaping social identities?
4. How has the shift to a knowledge-based economy impacted class structures?
5. In what ways does economic inequality affect access to healthcare?
6. What is the connection between economic growth and lifestyle choices in modern societies?

Long Answer Questions

1. Explain how the evolution from agrarian to industrial economies reshaped the social organization and the distribution of opportunities within society.

2. Discuss the impact of economic transitions on work and occupations, particularly the shift from manual labour to service- and knowledge-based jobs, and its effect on social mobility.

3. Analyse the role of consumption and digital access in shaping social status in modern societies. How has economic growth influenced consumption patterns?

4. Examine the consequences of economic inequality on political participation and social stability. How does inequality influence access to education and employment opportunities?

5. How have changing economic structures affected the social class system? Discuss the emerging divisions between high-skilled and low-skilled occupations in post-industrial economies.

6. Critically evaluate the social consequences of economic inequality in terms of healthcare access, education, and social integration. How can policies be designed to address these disparities?

4

Technology, Media, and the Digital Social Order

4.1 Technology as a Catalyst of Social Transformation

Technological development has become one of the most powerful forces shaping modern societies. Innovations in communication, transportation, and automation influence how people work, interact, and organize their daily lives.

Technological advancements have become a fundamental driver of societal change, reshaping virtually every aspect of human life. From the invention of the printing press to the rise of the internet, each technological leap has had profound effects on the way people live, work, and interact. In modern times, technology has accelerated social transformation by reducing physical and social distances, fostering more efficient systems, and creating new frameworks for understanding and solving problems.

One of the primary ways technologies has influenced society is through communication. The advent of the internet, mobile phones, and social media platforms has connected people across vast geographical distances, enabling instant communication and access to information. This interconnectedness has fostered global communities, allowed for the rapid spread of ideas, and created opportunities for collaboration and collective action that were previously unimaginable. For example, social movements such as the Arab Spring or environmental campaigns like #FridaysForFuture have been largely driven by digital platforms, illustrating how technology can empower individuals to mobilize for social causes.

Furthermore, technology has revolutionized transportation, reducing barriers to physical mobility and facilitating the global movement of people and goods. Innovations such as air travel, high-speed trains, and ride-sharing apps have not only made travel faster and more affordable but also contributed to the development of a more interconnected global economy. The ability to travel long distances quickly has reshaped the ways in which people live and work, enabling cross-border business operations and fostering cultural exchange.

Automation and artificial intelligence are other examples of technological advancements that are transforming industries and work structures. Machines and software are increasingly taking over tasks that were traditionally performed by humans, leading to increased productivity and efficiency in various sectors, including manufacturing, healthcare, and finance. While automation has the potential to improve economic outcomes, it also presents challenges, such as job displacement and the need for reskilling workers. Nevertheless, the integration of advanced technologies into everyday life continues to reshape societal structures, altering the workforce, economic models, and social interactions.

4.2 Media, Communication, and Social Interaction

Media plays a central role in shaping public opinion and social awareness. Digital platforms allow individuals to share information instantly, participate in public debates, and build virtual communities.

Media has always been a central force in shaping public opinion, influencing societal values, and defining how individuals interact with one another. In the digital age, media has taken on even greater significance, as technological innovations have expanded the ways in which people communicate and engage with information. Digital platforms, such as social media, blogs, podcasts, and news websites, have transformed traditional communication dynamics, allowing individuals to share ideas, participate in public discourse, and form online communities with ease.

One of the key contributions of digital media is its ability to provide instant access to information. Social media platforms like Twitter, Facebook, and Instagram enable individuals to share news, opinions, and personal experiences in real-time, making it possible to stay informed about local and global events almost immediately. This instant connectivity has brought about a more informed society, where people can access a vast array of viewpoints, learn about different cultures, and participate in real-time global conversations.

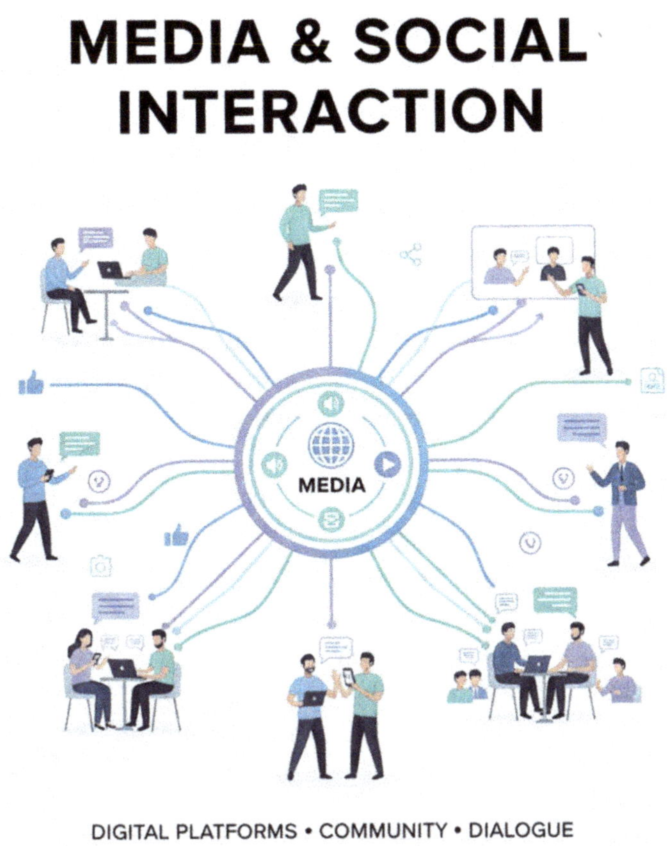

Additionally, media has played a pivotal role in democratizing information, allowing people from diverse backgrounds and regions to have a platform for their voices. It has given rise to virtual communities centred around shared interests, causes, and identities, enabling people to find support and solidarity from others they may never have encountered in person. These online communities have become important spaces for social interaction, as they allow individuals to exchange ideas, collaborate on projects, and advocate for social change.

Aspect	Positive Impacts	Challenges	Examples
Instant Information Access	Enables real-time sharing and access to news and updates.	Risk of misinformation and rapid spread of false news.	Social media platforms like Twitter for live news updates.
Democratization of Information	Gives people a platform to voice their opinions and share ideas.	Information overload, leading to confusion or stress.	Blogs, podcasts, and social media as platforms for various voices.
Virtual Communities	Facilitates the formation of online communities with shared interests and goals.	Reduced quality of real-world social interactions.	Online forums, support groups, and activism on platforms like Facebook.
Public Participation	Enhances public debate and collective decision-making.	Polarization, echo chambers, and division in society.	Political discussions on social media, crowdsourced content on platforms like Reddit.
Social Connectivity	Strengthens connections and allows long-distance communication.	Increased loneliness due to less face-to-face interaction.	Messaging apps, video calls, social media platforms for

			staying in touch.

However, despite the many benefits, the rise of digital media has also brought about several challenges. One of the most pressing concerns is the spread of misinformation. In a digital world where anyone can publish content, false or misleading information can spread quickly and widely, often reaching large audiences before it can be corrected. This has led to widespread debates about the responsibility of media platforms in curbing misinformation and the role of consumers in critically evaluating the information they encounter. The spread of fake news and the creation of echo chambers where people are exposed only to viewpoints that align with their own beliefs have contributed to increasing polarization, further dividing society along ideological lines.

4.3 Digital Inequality and Access to Technology

Despite technological progress, access to digital resources remains unequal. Differences in income, education, geography, and infrastructure create a digital divide that limits participation for certain groups.

While technological advancements have significantly enhanced connectivity and access to information, the benefits of these innovations are not equally distributed across all segments of society. Digital inequality refers to the disparities in access to digital technologies and the internet, which are influenced by factors such as income, education, geography, and infrastructure. These inequalities prevent certain groups from fully participating in the digital world, perpetuating existing social disparities and limiting opportunities for those who are already marginalized.

One of the primary drivers of digital inequality is income disparity. Individuals from lower-income households are less likely to own personal devices such as computers or smartphones, and they may have limited access to high-speed internet. This lack of access restricts their ability to participate in digital learning, work remotely, or access essential services that are increasingly offered online, such as healthcare consultations or government services. As a result, these individuals are often left behind in an increasingly digital world, unable to take advantage of opportunities that are critical for social mobility.

Educational differences also contribute to digital inequality. People with lower levels of formal education may lack the necessary skills to navigate digital tools effectively. Furthermore, they may not have the resources to participate in digital learning opportunities, such as online courses or e-learning platforms. This technological knowledge gap limits their ability to improve their skills or access higher-paying job opportunities that require digital literacy.

Geographic location plays a significant role in determining access to technology as well. Rural and remote areas, especially in developing countries, often face challenges in terms of infrastructure. Inadequate broadband connectivity, limited access to devices, and lower technological adoption rates in these areas create barriers to digital participation. In contrast, urban areas typically benefit from better internet infrastructure, making digital services and resources more accessible. This geographic divide further exacerbates the gap between urban and rural populations, contributing to unequal access to education, employment, and healthcare.

Infrastructure also plays a critical role in digital inequality. In many developing countries, unreliable electricity and poor telecommunication networks make it difficult for people to access or use digital technologies consistently. Even when individuals in these regions have access to digital devices, the lack of reliable infrastructure can undermine their ability to fully benefit from technological advances.

4.4 Ethical and Social Challenges of the Digital Age

The digital transformation introduces ethical challenges related to privacy, surveillance, and data security. Social dependence on technology also raises concerns about mental well-being and reduced face-to-face interaction.

The digital transformation has brought about significant advancements, enhancing communication, productivity, and access to information. However, alongside these benefits, it has also introduced complex ethical and social challenges that require careful consideration. Issues related to privacy, surveillance, data security, mental well-being, and social interaction have become central concerns in the digital age. These challenges highlight the need for responsible innovation and the development of regulatory frameworks that ensure the responsible use of technology, while safeguarding individual rights and societal well-being.

Privacy and Surveillance

As more personal information is shared and stored online, privacy has become a critical concern. Digital platforms, social media, and mobile applications collect vast amounts of data about individuals, including their behaviours, preferences, and locations. While this data can be used to personalize services, it also raises questions about who owns this information and how it is used. The unauthorized use or exploitation of personal data can lead to privacy violations, identity theft, and exploitation for commercial or political gain.

Data Security

With the increasing reliance on digital technologies, the security of data has become a major issue. Cyberattacks, data breaches, and hacking attempts are constant threats to the integrity of personal, corporate, and government data. Sensitive information, such as financial records, healthcare data, and personal identification details, are particularly vulnerable to theft and misuse. As technology evolves, so too do the methods used by cybercriminals, making it challenging for organizations to keep up with the latest security measures.

The loss or compromise of personal data can have severe consequences for individuals, leading to financial losses, reputational damage, and even physical harm in some cases. Therefore, ensuring robust data security measures and implementing encryption, authentication, and other protective technologies is essential for safeguarding users' privacy.

Mental Well-being and Social Interaction

While digital technologies offer numerous benefits, they also have a significant impact on mental health and social interaction. Social media platforms, in particular, can contribute to anxiety, depression, and feelings of inadequacy, especially among younger users. The constant exposure to curated and idealized images of others' lives can lead to social comparison, lowering self-esteem and fostering a distorted view of reality. The pressure to maintain an online persona or seek validation through likes and comments further exacerbates these issues.

Responsible Innovation and Digital Literacy

Addressing the ethical and social challenges of the digital age requires responsible innovation. Technology companies must prioritize ethical considerations when designing and deploying new products, ensuring that privacy, security, and social well-being are central to their development processes. This involves implementing transparent data usage policies, ensuring informed consent for data collection, and adopting privacy-friendly features by default.

In addition to responsible innovation, promoting digital literacy is essential to empowering individuals to navigate the digital landscape safely and responsibly. Educating users about the risks of online activities, such as recognizing phishing attacks, safeguarding personal information, and understanding their digital footprint, can help mitigate the negative impacts of technology. Furthermore, enhancing digital literacy can encourage more informed participation in online discourse and enable individuals to engage with technology in a more critical and mindful way.

Multiple Choice Questions (MCQs)

1. How has technology influenced social change in modern societies?

A) By reducing the need for social interaction
B) By increasing social stratification
C) By accelerating connectivity and efficiency in daily life
D) By limiting access to information

Answer: C) By accelerating connectivity and efficiency in daily life

2. What is the primary ethical concern associated with the collection of personal data by digital platforms?

A) Data being used to improve user experiences
B) Data privacy and user consent
C) Data encryption
D) Data sharing with third-party advertisers

Answer: B) Data privacy and user consent

3. What is one of the significant social challenges posed by digital media?

A) Increased social cohesion
B) Reduced face-to-face interaction leading to social isolation
C) Improved public discourse
D) Increased global collaboration

Answer: B) Reduced face-to-face interaction leading to social isolation

4. How does digital inequality impact access to education?

A) It provides equal access to all educational platforms
B) It creates barriers for individuals without access to technology, limiting their learning opportunities
C) It ensures that only the privileged have access to digital tools
D) It helps reduce educational disparities

Answer: B) It creates barriers for individuals without access to technology, limiting their learning opportunities

5. Which of the following is a major concern regarding digital media and mental well-being?

A) The ease of accessing educational resources
B) The potential for addiction and emotional stress from social media

C) The increase in face-to-face communication
D) The reduction of online content

Answer: B) The potential for addiction and emotional stress from social media

Short Answer Questions

1. How does technology act as a catalyst for social change in modern societies?
2. What role does digital media play in shaping public opinion?
3. What is the digital divide, and how does it impact marginalized groups?
4. What ethical issues arise from the use of personal data by digital platforms?
5. How has digital media contributed to the spread of misinformation?
6. What are the social implications of reduced face-to-face interactions due to increased digital communication?

Long Answer Questions

1. Explain how technology has transformed communication and social interaction in the digital age. Discuss both the positive and negative effects.
2. What are the key ethical and social challenges associated with the rise of digital platforms, and how can they be addressed to ensure responsible use of technology?
3. Discuss the impact of digital inequality on educational and employment opportunities. How can society bridge this digital divide?

4. Analyse the role of media in shaping societal norms and values. How has the digital transformation of media changed the way people perceive themselves and others?

5. Examine the consequences of data privacy violations in the digital age. Discuss a real-world example of a data breach and its impact on public trust.

6. Evaluate the effects of digital media on mental health and well-being. What steps can be taken to mitigate the negative effects of excessive media consumption?

5

Politics, Power, and Social Movements in a Changing World

5.1 Power, Authority, and Governance Structures

Power refers to the ability of individuals or institutions to influence social behaviour and decision-making. Modern governance structures are shaped by changing political ideologies, legal frameworks, and public expectations.

Power is the capacity of individuals, groups, or institutions to influence the actions, decisions, and behaviour of others within a society. It encompasses both the ability to enforce decisions and the influence over people's values, beliefs, and actions. In modern societies, power is often linked to various sources, including wealth, social status, control over information, and political influence. Institutions such as governments, corporations, and social organizations exercise power in different ways to shape public opinion, enforce laws, or dictate the terms of social interaction.

Authority, on the other hand, refers to the recognized legitimacy of power. It is the right or permission to make decisions, issue commands, or enforce obedience within a given domain. Authority often stems from the position someone holds in a hierarchy, such as that of a government official, a corporate leader, or a religious figure. However, unlike power, which can be wielded through force or coercion, authority is generally viewed as more legitimate, often supported by legal or social frameworks that grant individuals or institutions the right to exercise control.

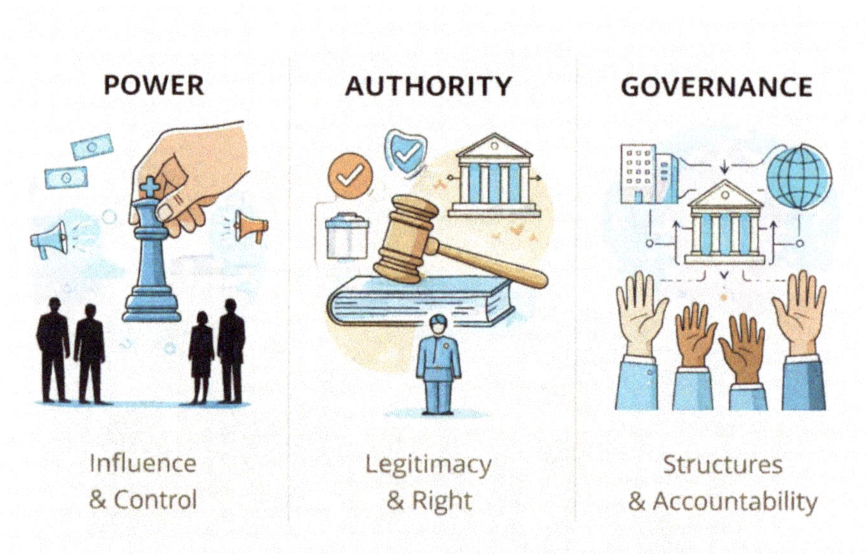

Governance structures in modern societies are constantly evolving, shaped by political ideologies, legal systems, and societal demands. In traditional societies, governance was often centralized, with power concentrated in a small group of elites or a single monarch. Over time, the expansion of democracy, the establishment of legal rights, and the influence of civil society have created more decentralized and complex governance systems. These modern structures aim to balance power across multiple actors, such as governments, citizens, businesses, and international organizations.

One significant feature of contemporary governance is the increasing scrutiny and demand for transparency and accountability. With the rise of social media and global communication networks, citizens are more informed and empowered to question authority, hold leaders accountable, and demand more responsive governance. This shift has led to the decline of some traditional forms of authority and the redefinition of political and corporate power dynamics. Today, the effectiveness of governance is often judged by how well it reflects the needs of the people it serves, ensuring both justice and fairness in decision-making processes.

5.2 Political Participation and Civic Engagement

Political participation extends beyond voting to include activism, public dialogue, and community organization. Increased access to information has encouraged citizens to become more involved in political processes. Civic engagement strengthens democracy by giving individuals a voice in shaping social policies and collective futures.

Political participation refers to the active involvement of individuals in the decision-making processes that shape their communities and countries. While voting is often seen as the most direct form of political participation, it extends far beyond that. Political participation includes activities such as activism, public dialogue, attending town hall meetings, lobbying, volunteering, and engaging in grassroots organizing. These activities allow individuals to express their views, advocate for change, and influence the policies and practices that govern their lives.

One of the key drivers of increased political participation is the growing access to information. In the digital age, the availability of news, political commentary, and data has made it easier for people to become informed about political issues. Social media platforms, blogs, podcasts, and online forums provide citizens with a wealth of information and a space to discuss current events and political matters. This ease of access has empowered more individuals to engage with political topics, share their opinions, and take action in ways that were not as feasible in the past.

Civic engagement, a subset of political participation, plays a crucial role in strengthening democracy. It ensures that individuals not only vote but also actively participate in the processes that shape social policies and public governance. By engaging with civic institutions and community organizations, people contribute to a more robust and inclusive democratic system. Civic engagement can take various forms, including volunteering in local organizations, participating in public consultations, or advocating for social issues. It empowers individuals to voice their concerns and be active agents in the creation of collective futures.

Moreover, increased civic engagement fosters a deeper sense of community and solidarity. When people come together to discuss issues, organize protests, or work on community projects, they not only influence policy but also strengthen the social fabric. This collaborative effort ensures that democratic institutions remain accountable and responsive to the needs of all citizens, regardless of their background or status. Ultimately, political participation and civic engagement are integral to the health of democracy, ensuring that power remains in the hands of the people and that their voices are heard in shaping the direction of society.

Aspect	Political Participation	Civic Engagement
Definition	Active involvement in political decision-making processes.	Participation in community or public activities to influence policies.
Key Activities	Voting, activism, public dialogue, community organizing.	Volunteering, attending public consultations, advocacy.
Primary Purpose	To influence political outcomes and governance.	To strengthen democracy and ensure social accountability.

Impact on Democracy	Ensures representative decision-making and policy change.	Fosters inclusivity, transparency, and community solidarity.
Examples	Voting in elections, lobbying, attending protests.	Volunteering in local organizations, participating in community meetings.
Drivers	Access to political information, social media, civic education.	Increased community involvement, awareness of social issues.

5.3 Social Movements as Agents of Change

Social movements emerge when groups mobilize to challenge injustice or demand reform. Movements related to civil rights, environmental protection, and social equality illustrate how collective action can influence laws, norms, and public consciousness. These movements reflect the dynamic relationship between society and political power.

Social movements are organized efforts by groups of people to bring about social, political, or environmental change. They often emerge in response to perceived injustices, inequalities, or the need for reform in society. These movements are typically driven by collective action, where individuals unite around shared grievances or goals. Through protests, advocacy, and activism, social movements seek to influence public policy, challenge existing power structures, and reshape social norms.

One of the defining features of social movements is their ability to mobilize large groups of people who are motivated by a common cause. Movements often arise in response to systemic issues, such as civil rights violations, environmental degradation, or social inequality. For example, the Civil Rights Movement in the United States sought to challenge racial segregation and discrimination against African Americans. Similarly, movements focused on environmental protection advocate for policies to combat climate change and preserve natural resources for future generations. Social movements related to gender equality, LGBTQ+ rights, and labour rights all serve as powerful examples of how collective action can demand reform and promote social justice.

Social movements are critical in shaping the public consciousness by drawing attention to issues that might otherwise be overlooked. By organizing protests, campaigns, and educational initiatives, they raise awareness and provoke dialogue among citizens, policymakers, and institutions. These movements create a sense of urgency around social issues, helping to foster a more informed and active public. They can also challenge dominant ideologies and highlight the struggles of marginalized or oppressed groups, ensuring that their voices are heard in political and social discussions.

The impact of social movements is also defined by the resistance they encounter. Every significant push for social change frequently triggers the emergence of counter-movements—organized efforts by those who seek to preserve the status quo or reverse the progress made by activists. This dynamic creates a "dialectic of change," where society undergoes a constant negotiation between reformist and conservative forces. Additionally, movements must navigate the risk of co-optation, where powerful institutions or corporations adopt the outward symbols and language of a movement to improve their public image without implementing meaningful structural or systemic changes.

Ultimately, the success of social movements is measured by their ability to institutionalize change through legal frameworks and shifts in cultural values. Beyond the immediate visibility of protests, the long-term victory of collective action is often found in new legislation, updated educational curricula, and the evolution of workplace policies. By continuously questioning the distribution of power and demanding accountability, social movements remain the primary engine for the expansion of human rights and the pursuit of a more equitable global society.

Aspect	Social Movements
Definition	Organized efforts by groups to challenge injustice or demand reform.
Primary Purpose	To bring about social, political, or environmental change.
Key Activities	Protests, advocacy, awareness campaigns, and activism.
Impact on Society	Influence laws, norms, and public consciousness.
Examples	Civil Rights Movement, Environmental Protection Movements, Feminist Movements.
Drivers	Grievances, collective action, societal inequalities.
Influence on Public Consciousness	Raise awareness and provoke dialogue on social issues.
Historical Impact	Led to significant reforms in civil rights, gender equality, and environmental policies.
Key Goal	To challenge and reform political systems and social norms.

5.4 Global Politics and Transnational Influences

Modern political change is increasingly influenced by global forces such as international organizations, economic alliances, and global public

opinion. Decisions made beyond national boundaries can impact local societies.

In today's interconnected world, modern political change is not solely driven by national forces but is increasingly shaped by global influences. These transnational forces include international organizations, economic alliances, and global public opinion, all of which transcend national borders and affect the governance and policies of individual countries. The actions and decisions of these global entities can have profound effects on local societies, influencing everything from economic policies to social norms and environmental practices.

International organizations such as the United Nations (UN), World Trade Organization (WTO), and World Health Organization (WHO) play a significant role in shaping global politics. These institutions provide platforms for dialogue and cooperation on a range of issues, from peace and security to trade and health. They set international standards, mediate conflicts, and offer assistance to countries in need. The policies and resolutions passed by such organizations can compel nations to adopt reforms, align with global norms, or face economic and diplomatic consequences.

Economic alliances and trade agreements, such as the European Union (EU), North American Free Trade Agreement (NAFTA), and the Trans-Pacific Partnership (TPP), further influence national policies. These alliances create interdependence among nations, fostering cooperation on economic matters and encouraging collective approaches to challenges like climate change, human rights, and global health crises. Decisions made within these economic blocs can drive political changes at the national level, as member countries must align their policies with the broader objectives of the alliance.

Global public opinion also plays a crucial role in modern political change. The rise of social media and the rapid spread of information have made it easier for global citizens to engage in political discourse and exert pressure on governments. Issues such as climate change, human rights, and global inequality are increasingly framed in global terms, and public opinion can influence national leaders to take action. For example, international protests, online campaigns, and global awareness efforts can compel governments to adopt policies in line with international expectations or risk international backlash.

Multiple Choice Questions (MCQs)

1. What is the primary role of social movements in modern society?

    a) To influence political leaders only
    b) To bring about social, political, or environmental change through collective action

c) To support the status quo and resist change
d) To establish centralized political systems

Answer: b) To bring about social, political, or environmental change through collective action

2. Which of the following is an example of political participation beyond voting?

a) Engaging in social media discussions
b) Watching political debates on television
c) Attending a political rally or protest
d) Listening to political podcasts

Answer: c) Attending a political rally or protest

3. How do international organizations like the United Nations (UN) influence global politics?

a) By enforcing national laws directly
b) By providing a platform for diplomatic dialogue and cooperation
c) By taking control of local government operations
d) By restricting individual freedoms within countries

Answer: b) By providing a platform for diplomatic dialogue and cooperation

4. What role does global public opinion play in modern political change?

a) It has no impact on political decision-making
b) It helps shape national policies by applying international pressure
c) It only affects the economic decisions of governments
d) It is used exclusively to influence corporate policies

Answer: b) It helps shape national policies by applying international pressure

5. What is one significant effect of social movements on public consciousness?

a) They isolate specific issues from the broader societal context
b) They raise awareness about important issues and challenge existing power structures
c) They promote the dominance of one social class over others
d) They prevent governments from making any reforms

Answer: b) They raise awareness about important issues and challenge existing power structures

Short Answer Questions

1. What is the difference between power and authority in political structures?
2. How do social movements contribute to shaping public policies?
3. What role do international organizations play in influencing national political decisions?
4. In what ways does global public opinion impact national governance?
5. What is the significance of civic engagement in a democratic society?
6. Explain the relationship between political participation and the strengthening of democracy.

Long Answer Questions

1. Discuss the concept of political participation beyond voting, and explain how it contributes to the political system. Provide examples of non-voting activities that help shape government policies.
2. Analyse the role of social movements in challenging social norms and political systems. How do movements like the Civil Rights Movement or environmental movements influence societal change and policy reform?

3. Examine how economic alliances, such as the European Union (EU), influence the political and economic decisions of member nations. What are the positive and negative impacts of such global economic partnerships on local governance?

4. Describe the dynamic relationship between political power and social movements. How do social movements challenge traditional political authority and power structures? Provide real-world examples of such movements.

5. Explore the impact of international organizations like the United Nations (UN) and World Trade Organization (WTO) on global political change. How do these organizations shape national policies in areas such as human rights, trade, and climate change?

6. Evaluate the role of global public opinion in influencing national policies on issues such as climate change, human rights, and social justice. How does the global community apply pressure on national governments to adopt international standards?

6

Family, Education, and Social Institutions in Transition

6.1 Changing Family Structures and Relationships

Family structures have diversified due to urbanization, changing gender roles, and economic pressures. Nuclear families, single-parent households, and shared caregiving arrangements reflect shifting social values. These changes influence socialization, emotional support systems, and intergenerational relationships.

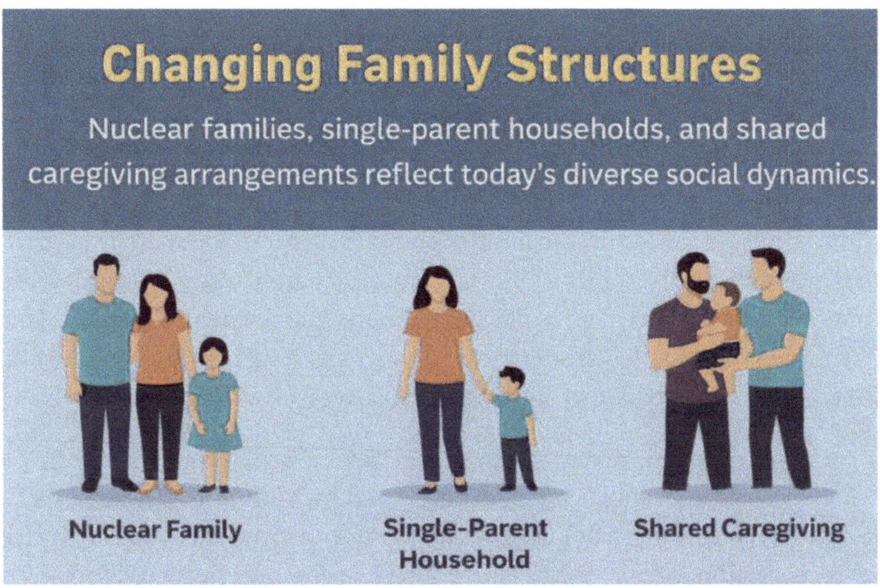

The concept of family has evolved significantly in modern societies, driven by various social, economic, and cultural factors. Traditionally, family structures were more stable and predominantly consisted of extended families where multiple generations coexisted under one roof. However, with urbanization, the dynamics of family life have changed, leading to a rise in diverse family configurations.

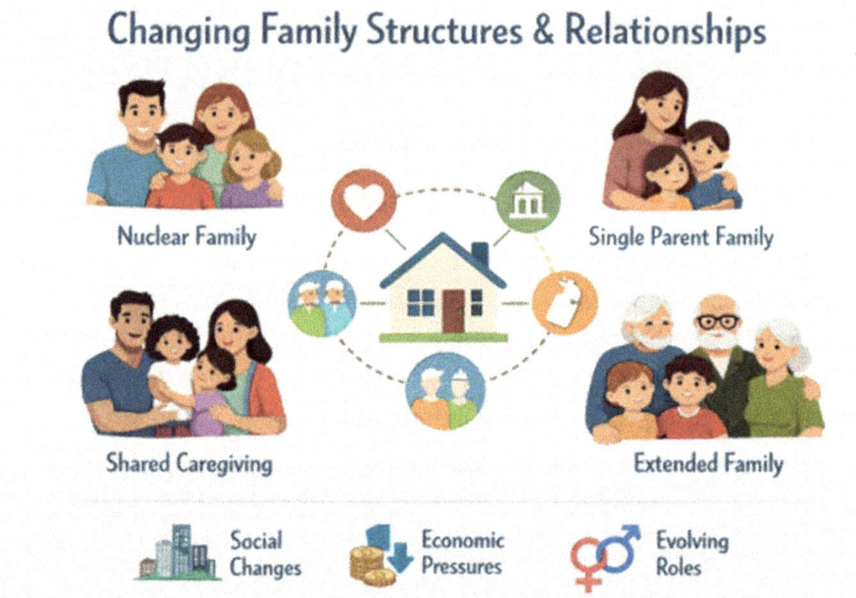

One of the most notable changes is the growth of nuclear families. The shift from joint families to nuclear families-comprising parents and their children-has been influenced by factors like migration for better job opportunities, the pursuit of education, and a desire for more independent lifestyles. This transformation has led to significant changes in how families interact and function, as the extended network of relatives providing emotional and financial support is often no longer present.

Single-parent households are another important shift in family structures. Economic pressures, changing societal norms, and increasing rates of divorce and separation have contributed to a rise in families headed by a single parent, often the mother. Single-parent families face unique challenges, such as balancing work and caregiving responsibilities, and they may lack the extended familial support that was once typical. These families are more likely to experience economic hardship, but they also foster a sense of resilience and independence in both parents and children.

Shared caregiving arrangements, particularly among same-sex couples and unmarried partners, are increasingly common. These arrangements highlight a broader definition of family that is less concerned with traditional gender roles and more focused on mutual support and caregiving. These non-traditional family structures can have different emotional dynamics and raise questions about legal recognition, social acceptance, and the evolving definition of family in modern society.

The shifting nature of family structures also influences how individuals experience socialization and emotional support. In nuclear and single-parent families, children may experience a different kind of upbringing compared to those in extended families, as their interactions with a wider network of relatives become less frequent. This can impact emotional development, with children in smaller family units potentially having closer bonds with immediate family members but less exposure to intergenerational relationships. Additionally, the role of grandparents in providing care, teaching, and emotional support may be diminished, further altering the ways in which individuals are socialized and develop relational skills.

6.2 Education as a Tool for Social Mobility

Education plays a crucial role in shaping social opportunities and individual aspirations. Expanding access to education has enabled greater social mobility, while inequalities in educational quality continue to reinforce social stratification. Education also transmits cultural values and prepares individuals for participation in modern societies.

Education is often regarded as one of the most powerful tools for fostering social mobility, as it provides individuals with the skills, knowledge, and credentials necessary to improve their socio-economic status. By broadening access to learning opportunities, education can open doors to better employment, higher income, and enhanced quality of life, ultimately helping to reduce inequalities and bridge social divides.

Historically, education has been a means for individuals from disadvantaged backgrounds to rise above their social class. By acquiring literacy, vocational training, and higher education, individuals can secure employment in more skilled and higher-paying sectors, thus improving their living standards. Education, in this sense, serves as a key equalizer by providing people with the tools they need to compete in the labour market and pursue career advancement, regardless of their social origin. As a result, education is often seen as a pathway to breaking the cycle of poverty and achieving upward social mobility.

However, despite its potential to promote social mobility, education systems around the world are often marked by significant disparities in quality. Inequities in educational resources, infrastructure, and access to skilled teachers can reinforce existing social stratification, rather than challenge it. For example, children from affluent families typically attend well-funded schools with access to advanced learning materials, extracurricular activities, and a robust support system, whereas those from lower-income families may be relegated to underfunded schools with fewer opportunities. These differences in educational quality can perpetuate a cycle of inequality, where the rich have access to superior education that further solidifies their social and economic advantages, while the poor remain disadvantaged.

In addition to facilitating economic mobility, education also plays a critical role in transmitting cultural values and norms. Schools and universities are not just sites for academic learning, but also places where individuals are socialized into the values, behaviours, and expectations of the broader society. Through curricula, interactions with peers, and exposure to different ideologies, education helps shape the ways individuals view the world and their role within it. It prepares individuals for active participation in civic life, instilling a sense of belonging and responsibility to the community, fostering critical thinking, and encouraging informed decision-making.

6.3 Social Institutions and Adaptation to Change

Institutions such as religion, healthcare, and law adapt to changing social realities. Reforms in institutional practices often respond to demographic

shifts, technological advancements, and cultural diversity. Institutional flexibility is essential for maintaining social stability during periods of rapid change.

Social institutions, such as religion, healthcare, and law, play a crucial role in maintaining order and ensuring the functioning of society. However, these institutions are not static; they must adapt to meet the challenges posed by shifting social dynamics, including demographic changes, technological advancements, and cultural diversity. The ability of institutions to evolve in response to these changes is essential for ensuring that they continue to serve the needs of society while maintaining social stability.

1. Adaptation in Religion

Religion has historically been a cornerstone of societal values and norms, guiding moral conduct and offering a sense of community. However, as societies become more diverse and secular, religious institutions have been forced to adapt. For example, many religious organizations are increasingly addressing contemporary issues such as gender equality, LGBTQ+ rights, and environmental sustainability. In some cases, traditional interpretations of religious doctrines have evolved, allowing for more inclusive practices and a broader appeal to a changing demographic.

2. Adaptation in Healthcare

Healthcare systems are another example of institutions that must adapt to demographic shifts and technological advancements. As populations age, there is a growing demand for healthcare services tailored to the needs of older adults. Healthcare providers are increasingly focusing on chronic disease management, palliative care, and geriatric services to address this shift.

Technological advancements, such as telemedicine, electronic health records, and robotic surgery, are also transforming the healthcare sector. These innovations improve patient care, increase accessibility, and streamline administrative processes. However, the integration of new technologies into healthcare systems requires ongoing adaptation to ensure that ethical standards are maintained and that healthcare remains accessible to all, especially marginalized communities.

3. Adaptation in Law

Legal systems, like other social institutions, must also evolve in response to societal changes. Legal reforms often occur in response to shifts in social values, technological advancements, and demographic changes. For example, as societies become more diverse and inclusive, legal systems have adapted by enacting laws that protect against discrimination based on gender, race, ethnicity, and sexual orientation.

The advent of new technologies has also brought about the need for legal reforms in areas such as data privacy, intellectual property, and cybersecurity. As more personal and professional activities move online, legal frameworks must adapt to address new risks and challenges associated with digital technologies. Laws surrounding artificial intelligence, data protection, and the ethical use of emerging technologies are critical in maintaining justice and fairness in the modern world.

Moreover, as demographic patterns change, legal systems may also need to adjust to accommodate an aging population or shifting immigration trends. This could involve reforms in areas like elder law, immigration policy, and workers' rights, ensuring that the legal system reflects the evolving needs of society.

6.4 Socialization and Value Transmission in Modern Society

Socialization is the process through which individuals learn social norms and values. In modern societies, socialization occurs through family, education, media, and peer groups. As these agents evolve, the ways values are transmitted also change, influencing identity formation and social cohesion.

Socialization is the process by which individuals learn and internalize the norms, values, and behaviours that are expected in their society. This process begins in childhood and continues throughout life, shaping how individuals understand their roles within the family, community, and broader society. In modern societies, socialization occurs through various agents, including the family, education, media, and peer groups. These agents play a significant role in transmitting societal values and norms, influencing identity formation and social cohesion.

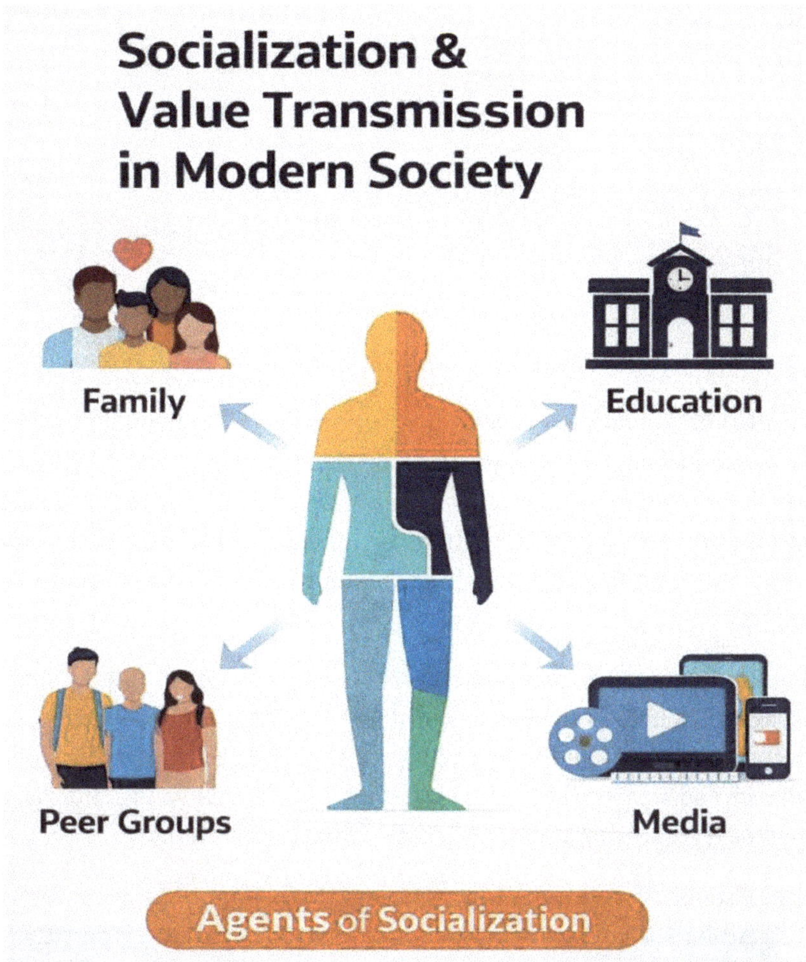

Key Agents of Socialization:

1. **Family** : The family is the primary agent of socialization, especially in early childhood. It provides the first exposure to social norms, language, and

emotional development. Parents and caregivers instil values such as respect, responsibility, and cultural traditions, which become the foundation for how children perceive the world and interact with others.

2. **Education**: Schools are formal institutions where individuals learn not only academic knowledge but also social norms and values. Education systems teach students about social roles, citizenship, and cultural values. They also promote social integration, as students from diverse backgrounds interact and learn together, helping to foster a sense of shared identity and belonging.

3. **Media**: In contemporary society, media plays a central role in shaping values and beliefs. Television, social media, films, and advertisements influence how people view themselves, others, and the world around them. Media acts as a powerful tool for transmitting cultural values, norms, and trends, often reflecting and reinforcing societal expectations.

4. **Peer Groups**: Peer groups become increasingly important in adolescence and adulthood. These groups provide individuals with the opportunity to develop social skills, form personal identities, and navigate social pressures. Peer groups often influence behaviours, fashion, language, and attitudes, shaping how individuals conform to or challenge societal norms.

Changing Methods of Value Transmission:

As modern society evolves, so too do the methods of value transmission. Technological advancements, particularly in digital media, have introduced new ways for values to be communicated. Social media platforms, online communities, and digital influencers have become significant sources of value transmission, particularly for younger generations. This shift has led to the emergence of new norms, often challenging traditional values while promoting diversity, individualism, and global interconnectedness.

Impact on Identity Formation and Social Cohesion:

The way values are transmitted through these agents of socialization influences how individuals form their identities. In modern societies, individuals are exposed to a wider variety of cultural norms and values, which can lead to more complex and fluid identities. This diversity of influences can either promote social cohesion by fostering understanding and tolerance or create tensions as individuals struggle to reconcile conflicting values.

Multiple Choice Questions (MCQs)

1. Which of the following is considered the primary agent of socialization, especially in early childhood?

A) Media

B) Peer Groups

C) Education

D) Family

Answer: D) Family

2. What is the main purpose of education in the context of socialization?

A) To impart academic knowledge only

B) To reinforce family values

C) To teach societal norms, values, and citizenship

D) To segregate individuals based on ability

Answer: C) To teach societal norms, values, and citizenship

3. Which of the following social agents has seen a significant increase in influence due to the rise of digital technologies and social media?

A) Family

B) Education

C) Media

D) Peer Groups

Answer: C) Media

4. How has the shift to nuclear families affected socialization in modern societies?

A) It has no impact on socialization.

B) It has reduced the diversity of social influences.

C) It has led to more individualized socialization.

D) It has increased the role of extended families in socialization.

Answer: C) It has led to more individualized socialization.

5. In contemporary societies, which of the following is a significant result of the evolving methods of value transmission through digital media?

A) Decreased exposure to global cultures

B) Strengthened traditional values and norms

C) Creation of new norms and values, often challenging traditional ones

D) Social isolation of younger generations

Answer: C) Creation of new norms and values, often challenging traditional ones

Short Answer Questions

1. What is the role of family in the socialization process?
2. How do media influence the transmission of cultural values in modern society?
3. Explain the impact of peer groups on identity formation during adolescence.
4. What is the significance of education in promoting social cohesion?
5. How have changes in family structures, like the rise of nuclear families, influenced socialization patterns?
6. What are the key challenges faced by social institutions in adapting to technological advancements?

Long Answer Questions

1. Discuss the role of education as an agent of socialization. How does it help individuals integrate into society while promoting social mobility?
2. Explain how digital media has transformed the way values and norms are transmitted to younger generations. What are the benefits and challenges associated with this shift?
3. Evaluate the changing role of religion in modern societies. How have religious institutions adapted to societal shifts, such as gender equality and cultural diversity?
4. Examine the effects of family structure changes, such as the rise of single-parent households and shared caregiving arrangements, on socialization and intergenerational relationships.

5. Analyse the concept of social cohesion in the context of evolving social institutions. How do education, law, and healthcare contribute to maintaining social stability during periods of rapid change?

6. Discuss the role of peer groups in shaping an individual's social identity. How do peer groups influence behaviours, values, and attitudes in modern society?

7

Globalization, Migration, and Cross-Cultural Interactions

7.1 Globalization and Interconnected Societies

Globalization refers to the growing interdependence of societies through trade, communication, technology, and cultural exchange. Economic integration and digital connectivity have reduced geographical boundaries, allowing ideas, goods, and practices to circulate rapidly.

Globalization has fundamentally transformed the way societies interact, both on a global and local scale. It is characterized by the increasing interconnectedness of countries through various channels such as trade, technology, communication, and cultural exchange. This process has facilitated the flow of goods, services, information, and ideas, breaking down the traditional barriers of geography and fostering a more integrated world.

One of the key aspects of globalization is **economic integration**, where countries are no longer isolated in terms of trade and industry. Global markets have led to greater economic cooperation, with nations depending on each other for goods, labour, and resources. International trade agreements, digital currencies, and multinational corporations have all played a role in knitting the world's economies together. This interconnectedness promotes efficiency, lowers costs, and drives innovation as countries share technology and expertise.

Digital connectivity is another crucial component of globalization. The internet and mobile communication have revolutionized how individuals and businesses operate. Social media platforms, online markets, and collaborative tools enable people to communicate, collaborate, and conduct business across borders instantaneously. For example, digital platforms like Amazon and Alibaba allow consumers in one country to purchase products from sellers in another, enabling a level of global trade previously unimaginable.

However, the rapid pace of globalization comes with its challenges. **Cultural homogenization** is a significant concern, as the dominance of global brands, media, and Western lifestyles can lead to the erosion of local cultures, languages, and traditions. The global spread of consumer culture often leads to the marginalization of indigenous practices and values, raising concerns about cultural diversity and identity preservation.

7.2 Migration and Social Transformation

Migration-both internal and international-plays a crucial role in reshaping social structures. Migrants contribute to demographic change, labour markets, and cultural diversity in host societies. At the same time, migration raises questions of integration, identity, and access to resources.

Migration, whether internal or international, is a powerful force driving social transformation in societies across the world. It contributes to shifts in **demographic structures** , **labour markets** , and **cultural diversity** , but it also brings forth significant challenges related to **integration**, **identity**, and **access to resources** .

One of the key impacts of migration is its **demographic influence** . As individuals and families move from rural to urban areas or from one country to another, they alter the composition of populations in both sending and receiving regions. Internal migration, such as rural-to-urban movement, often leads to the growth of cities and towns, changing the age, ethnicity, and socio-economic makeup of these areas. Similarly, international migration can significantly alter the demographic profile of a country, as seen in countries with high rates of immigration.

In terms of **labour markets** , migrants often fill essential roles in both developed and developing economies. Migrants contribute to the economy by providing labour in various sectors such as agriculture, construction, manufacturing, and service industries. For example, migrant workers often take jobs that are in high demand but are shunned by the local workforce. This can lead to increased productivity and economic growth in the host society. Additionally, migration can result in the transfer of skills and knowledge, enriching the labour market with diverse talents.

Migration also fosters **cultural diversity** in host societies. The introduction of new customs, traditions, cuisines, and languages can enhance cultural richness and innovation. Over time, this blending of cultures can lead to more inclusive societies that embrace diversity. However, it can also create tensions as the presence of migrant groups challenges existing cultural norms and raises questions about the balance between maintaining national identity and embracing multiculturalism.

Despite the benefits of migration, it also brings about significant **challenges of integration**. As migrants arrive in new regions, they often face difficulties in adjusting to unfamiliar social norms, economic systems, and political structures. In many cases, they encounter obstacles such as discrimination, limited access to social services, and the struggle to establish a sense of belonging. These challenges can lead to **social exclusion** and **segregation**,

7.3 Multiculturalism and Cultural Exchange

Cross-cultural interaction encourages the blending of traditions, languages, and lifestyles. Multicultural societies benefit from diversity through creativity and broader worldviews. However, successful multiculturalism depends on mutual respect and inclusive policies that prevent marginalization.

Cross-cultural interaction is one of the most dynamic forces in shaping modern societies. As people from diverse cultural backgrounds interact, they bring together a wide range of **traditions**, **languages**, and **lifestyles**, creating opportunities for the **blending of cultures**. This cultural exchange not only enriches societies but also promotes a deeper **understanding** of different ways of life.

One of the major benefits of **multiculturalism** is the infusion of **creativity** and **innovation** that arises when diverse cultural perspectives come together. In multicultural societies, individuals often draw on a variety of traditions, beliefs, and artistic expressions, leading to new forms of artistic, literary, and technological innovation. The exchange of ideas fosters creative thinking, adaptability, and problem-solving, enabling societies to become more resilient and dynamic in the face of global challenges. Additionally, **broader worldviews** emerge as individuals gain exposure to a wide array of cultural practices, expanding their understanding of global issues and promoting a sense of global citizenship.

Educational institutions that promote multiculturalism play a vital role in reducing prejudice and fostering greater social cohesion. By integrating

multicultural curricula , schools help students engage with diverse cultural perspectives, understand different histories, and develop **intercultural competence**. This not only improves the academic experience but also contributes to the development of empathy, tolerance, and respect for others. For instance, universities and schools that offer courses on world literature, global history, or cross-cultural communication provide students with tools to understand and appreciate cultural differences, equipping them to thrive in an increasingly interconnected world.

7.4 Challenges of Global Interdependence

Global interconnectedness can intensify inequalities between regions and nations. Economic dependency, cultural dominance, and uneven development create tensions within and across societies. Addressing these challenges requires cooperation, ethical globalization, and policies that prioritize social equity.

Global interconnectedness has brought societies closer, fostering unprecedented opportunities for economic growth, cultural exchange, and technological advancement. However, this **interdependence** has also led to **inequalities** that often disproportionately affect certain regions, nations, and social groups. As countries become more interconnected, the risks of **economic dependency**, **cultural dominance**, and **uneven development** intensify, creating significant challenges that need to be addressed for a fairer and more just global order.

One of the most pressing challenges of global interdependence is the **economic dependency** of developing nations on developed economies. Many countries rely heavily on exports of raw materials or low-cost labour to the industrialized world, leaving them vulnerable to fluctuations in global markets. This creates an imbalance where wealthier nations benefit from cheap resources or labour while the developing world struggles with poverty, limited infrastructure, and poor social services. As a result, economic dependency reinforces existing **global inequalities**, making it difficult for poorer countries to achieve sustainable development or economic independence.

Another issue arising from global interdependence is **cultural dominance**. The flow of global media, brands, and ideologies often Favors Western ideals, leading to a process known as **cultural imperialism**. Global media networks, multinational corporations, and international organizations tend to promote Western values, products, and lifestyles, overshadowing local cultures and traditions. This can result in the **erosion of indigenous cultures**, languages, and practices, as well as increased **social homogeneity**, where local populations adopt foreign values and customs to align with global trends. The influence of global culture can marginalize regional cultures, creating a sense of loss and disconnection within local communities.

Uneven development is another significant consequence of global interdependence. While some regions experience rapid economic growth due to globalization, others lag behind, exacerbating disparities between nations and within countries. Regions that are less integrated into global trade networks, or those that face political instability, may struggle to catch up with wealthier nations. Even within countries, globalization can lead to urban-rural divides, with urban centres benefiting from foreign investment and job creation, while rural areas experience stagnation or decline. This

uneven development contributes to widening **socio-economic gaps**, limiting opportunities for millions of people and leading to increased tensions within societies.

Addressing these challenges requires a concerted effort toward **cooperation** and the promotion of **ethical globalization**. Multilateral organizations such as the United Nations, World Trade Organization, and regional alliances must work together to ensure that globalization benefits all nations equitably. **Trade agreements** should prioritize fair terms for developing countries, and international investment should aim to bolster local industries and infrastructure rather than exploit resources for short-term profit. **Cultural exchange** must be promoted in a way that respects and preserves the diversity of traditions and practices, encouraging a balance between global influence and local identity.

Multiple Choice Questions (MCQs)

1. What is the primary benefit of globalization in terms of cultural exchange?

A) Economic dependency
B) Cultural homogenization
C) Enhancement of creativity and innovation
D) Erosion of local traditions

Answer: C) Enhancement of creativity and innovation

2. Which of the following is a common challenge faced by cities experiencing rural-to-urban migration?

A) Decreased pressure on public services
B) Improved housing conditions
C) Overcrowding and strain on infrastructure
D) Economic growth in rural areas

Answer: C) Overcrowding and strain on infrastructure

3. What does cultural dominance in globalization typically lead to?

A) Strengthening of local traditions
B) Emergence of global cultural diversity
C) Marginalization of indigenous cultures
D) Economic prosperity in all societies

Answer: C) Marginalization of indigenous cultures

4. Which of the following is an example of a benefit of multiculturalism?

A) Creation of economic dependency
B) Increased social segregation
C) Fostering creativity and innovation through diversity
D) Suppression of cultural identities

Answer: C) Fostering creativity and innovation through diversity

5. What key factor is essential for the success of multiculturalism in societies?

A) Cultural assimilation
B) Mutual respect and inclusive policies
C) Economic isolation
D) Cultural homogeneity

Answer: B) Mutual respect and inclusive policies

Short Answer Questions

1. What is the primary driver of global interconnectedness in modern societies?
2. How does rural-to-urban migration impact urban infrastructure?
3. What role does multicultural education play in reducing social prejudice?
4. Explain the concept of cultural homogenization in the context of globalization.

5. How does migration contribute to economic growth in host societies?

6. Why is mutual respect crucial for the success of multiculturalism?

Long Answer Questions

1. Discuss the impact of globalization on local cultures and the risks of cultural dominance. What measures can societies take to preserve cultural diversity while embracing globalization?

2. Examine the relationship between migration and social transformation. How do migrants contribute to demographic, economic, and cultural changes in host societies, and what challenges do they face in terms of integration?

3. Analyse the role of education in fostering intercultural understanding.

4. Explore the challenges of uneven development resulting from globalization.

5. Explain how the migration of people from rural to urban areas affects both the rural and urban economies.

8

Inequality, Social Justice, and Emerging Divides

8.1 Understanding Social Inequality

Social inequality refers to unequal access to resources, opportunities, and privileges within society. These inequalities are often structured around class, gender, ethnicity, and education. Persistent inequality limits social mobility and weakens social cohesion.

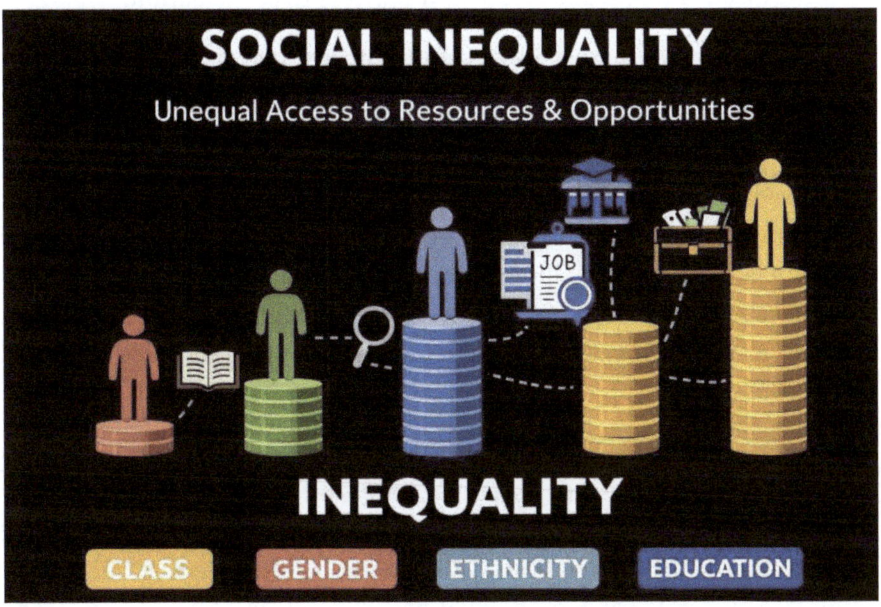

Social inequality refers to the unequal distribution of resources, opportunities, and privileges across different groups within society. It manifests in various forms, including economic, social, and political disparities. Inequality is often structured along axes such as class, gender, ethnicity, and education. These differences create systemic barriers that limit individuals' opportunities to succeed and thrive.

Social inequality can limit social mobility, meaning that individuals from disadvantaged backgrounds face significant challenges in improving their circumstances. This leads to a cycle of poverty and limited opportunities, which can persist across generations. For instance, children from lower-income families may not have access to quality education, which hinders their ability to acquire skills and secure well-paying jobs in the future.

8.2 Dimensions of Inequality in Modern Societies

Inequality is multidimensional, encompassing economic, social, and digital divides. Modern societies face new forms of exclusion, such as unequal access to technology and information. These divides reinforce existing disadvantages and create new barriers to participation.

Inequality in modern societies is multidimensional, involving not only economic disparities but also social, educational, and digital divides. These various forms of inequality compound one another, reinforcing existing disadvantages and creating new barriers to full participation in society.

1. **Economic Inequality** : Economic disparities are the most visible and traditional form of inequality, often manifesting in income differences, wealth gaps, and unequal access to essential resources like healthcare, housing, and food. This type of inequality limits upward social mobility and entrenches poverty.

2. **Social Inequality** : Social inequality is reflected in unequal opportunities based on social factors such as gender, race, and ethnicity. Discriminatory practices and biases can restrict access to opportunities, perpetuating disadvantage across generations. Women and marginalized ethnic groups often face systemic barriers to equal participation in social, political, and economic life.

3. **Digital Inequality** : The digital divide is a newer form of inequality that has become particularly apparent in recent years. It refers to the unequal access

to technology and digital resources, including the internet and information technologies. In an increasingly digital world, those without access to these resources are at a severe disadvantage, particularly in education, employment, and civic participation.

8.3 Social Justice Movements and Policy Responses

Social justice movements seek to challenge inequality and promote fairness. Through advocacy, awareness, and collective action, these movements influence public policy and social attitudes.

Social justice movements play a crucial role in challenging inequality and promoting fairness in society. These movements work to address disparities by advocating for the rights of marginalized groups, raising awareness, and pushing for systemic change. Their impact is often seen in the form of legal reforms, policy changes, and shifts in public attitudes.

1. **Advocacy and Collective Action** : Social justice movements are driven by collective action, where groups of people come together to challenge societal injustices. These movements often bring attention to issues such as racial discrimination, gender inequality, and income disparity, demanding change through protests, campaigns, and lobbying efforts. By uniting people around a common cause, social justice movements can amplify voices that would otherwise go unheard.

2. **Influencing Public Policy** : Over time, sustained advocacy by social justice movements leads to changes in public policy. These movements exert pressure on governments to adopt new laws or modify existing ones, aiming to eliminate discriminatory practices and create more equitable systems. This often involves direct engagement with policymakers and public officials to push for reforms that address the root causes of inequality.

3. **Legal Reforms and Welfare Programs** : As a response to social pressure, governments may implement legal reforms and welfare programs designed to reduce inequalities. These reforms are intended to level the playing field by ensuring equal access to resources and opportunities, such as education,

healthcare, and employment. Welfare programs may focus on providing financial support, healthcare, or housing to disadvantaged groups.

8.4 Toward Inclusive and Equitable Societies

Building inclusive societies requires addressing root causes of inequality rather than only its symptoms. Inclusive development emphasizes participation, representation, and equitable resource distribution. Long-term social stability depends on ensuring dignity and opportunity for all members of society.

Building inclusive societies requires more than just addressing the symptoms of inequality; it necessitates tackling the root causes that perpetuate these disparities. Inclusive development focuses on creating systems that allow everyone, regardless of their background, to participate fully in social, economic, and political life. Achieving this involves addressing the structural barriers that limit opportunities and ensuring that all members of society have access to resources, representation, and dignity.

1. **Addressing Root Causes of Inequality** : True inclusivity begins by understanding and dismantling the systems and structures that create inequality. This involves confronting historical and systemic factors such as racism, sexism, caste discrimination, and economic exploitation that limit opportunities for marginalized groups. By focusing on the root causes, inclusive policies can create sustainable change that prevents inequalities from re-emerging.

2. **Participation and Representation** : Inclusive societies promote the active participation of all individuals in decision-making processes. This means ensuring that people from diverse backgrounds-whether based on gender, ethnicity, disability, or socioeconomic status-have a voice in shaping policies that affect their lives. Representation in political, economic, and cultural institutions is essential for ensuring that the needs of all groups are met and that no one is left behind.

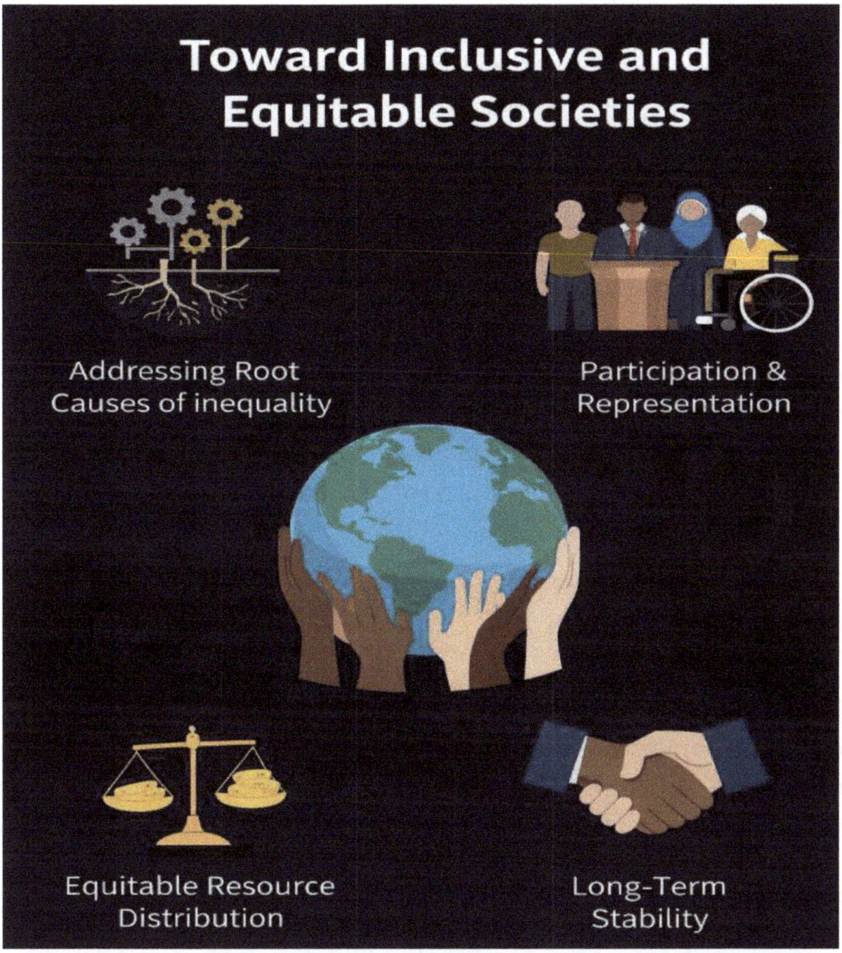

Key Aspect	Description	Examples
Addressing Root Causes of Inequality	Tackling the systemic factors (e.g., racism, sexism, economic exploitation) that perpetuate inequality.	Reforming policies to dismantle discriminatory structures such as caste-based practices or gender-based wage gaps.
Participation and Representation	Ensuring active involvement and representation of	Implementing affirmative action policies or quotas to ensure diverse

	marginalized groups in decision-making processes.	representation in political offices or corporate boards.
Equitable Resource Distribution	Providing equal access to resources like education, healthcare, and economic opportunities.	Expanding access to public education, healthcare, and job training programs in underdeveloped regions or communities.
Long-Term Social Stability	Ensuring that all members of society are given dignity and the opportunity to thrive.	Creating social safety nets, such as universal healthcare or welfare programs, that support vulnerable populations, contributing to social cohesion.

3. **Equitable Resource Distribution** : Ensuring that resources are distributed equitably is a cornerstone of inclusive development. This includes providing equal access to education, healthcare, employment, and economic opportunities. Equitable distribution ensures that all individuals, regardless of their background, can fulfil their potential and contribute to society, thereby fostering social cohesion and reducing disparities.

4. **Long-Term Social Stability** : Long-term stability within a society is rooted in the dignity and opportunity provided to all its members. Inclusive development not only focuses on immediate needs but also prioritizes creating a society where everyone has the opportunity to thrive, thus preventing social unrest and promoting harmony. When all individuals are valued and given equal opportunities, society as a whole becomes more resilient and stable.

By addressing inequality at its roots and focusing on inclusive development, societies can work toward greater fairness, stability, and long-term social progress. This holistic approach ensures that every individual can contribute to and benefit from the opportunities society has to offer.

Multiple Choice Questions (MCQs)

1. What is the primary focus of social justice movements?

A) To maintain the status quo in society

B) To challenge inequality and promote fairness

C) To eliminate all forms of governance

D) To increase wealth disparity in society

Answer: B) To challenge inequality and promote fairness

2. Which of the following is a major factor contributing to social inequality?

A) Equal access to healthcare

B) Disparities based on gender, race, and education

C) Universal access to technology

D) Widespread access to voting rights

Answer: B) Disparities based on gender, race, and education

3. Which of the following is an example of a digital divide in modern societies?

A) Unequal access to renewable energy

B) Lack of internet access for remote learning during the COVID-19 pandemic

C) Unequal distribution of agricultural resources

D) Barriers to public transportation access

Answer: B) Lack of internet access for remote learning during the COVID-19 pandemic

4. Which of the following is a key objective of inclusive development?

A) Focusing solely on economic growth without addressing social disparities

B) Ensuring that everyone has equal access to opportunities and resources

C) Prioritizing the needs of urban populations over rural populations

D) Promoting technological advancement without concern for social equity

Answer: B) Ensuring that everyone has equal access to opportunities and resources

5. What is the ultimate goal of addressing the root causes of inequality in society?

A) To create a system where only a few benefit

B) To maintain existing social structures and preserve traditional hierarchies

C) To build a society where all individuals have dignity and the opportunity to thrive

D) To increase the power of the elite class in society

Answer: C) To build a society where all individuals have dignity and the opportunity to thrive

Short Answer Questions

1. What is social justice?

2. How does the digital divide contribute to inequality in modern societies?
3. What role do social justice movements play in influencing policy reforms?
4. Give an example of how economic inequality affects access to education.
5. What is the significance of addressing the root causes of inequality?
6. How do inclusive societies promote long-term social stability?

Long Answer Questions

1. Explain the concept of social justice and discuss how social justice movements challenge inequality and promote fairness in society. Provide examples of successful movements that have led to policy reforms.
2. Discuss the different dimensions of inequality in modern societies, including economic, social, and digital divides. How do these forms of inequality reinforce each other and contribute to social exclusion?
3. In what ways can addressing the root causes of inequality lead to a more inclusive and equitable society? Provide examples of policies or actions that have successfully reduced systemic inequalities.
4. Analyse the role of technology in both exacerbating and addressing inequality. How does the digital divide impact access to opportunities, and what measures can be taken to ensure equal access to technology?
5. Discuss the importance of representation and participation in creating inclusive societies. How can ensuring diverse representation in political, economic, and social institutions help reduce inequalities?

6. Evaluate the long-term effects of social justice movements on creating equitable societies. How do legal reforms, welfare programs, and shifts in public attitudes contribute to reducing structural inequalities in society?

9

The Future of Social Change – Continuity, Adaptation, and Resilience

9.1 Patterns of Continuity and Change

Not all aspects of society change at the same pace. While some traditions persist, others adapt to new realities. Understanding this balance between continuity and change helps explain how societies maintain identity while evolving.

Patterns of continuity and change refer to the way societies maintain certain traditions while simultaneously adapting to new influences over time. Some aspects of society, such as cultural norms, values, and practices, remain stable, while others evolve in response to technological advancements, social shifts, or global interactions. This dual process of maintaining continuity and embracing change allows societies to preserve their identity while remaining open to growth and transformation.

Aspect	Description	Example
Continuity	The persistence of certain cultural or social elements over time.	Traditional community rituals (e.g., festivals)
Change	The adaptation or transformation of social, cultural, or technological practices.	Integration of modern technology in rituals (e.g., live-streaming festivals)
Balance Between Both	Maintaining core traditions while evolving to meet contemporary needs.	Festivals using social media for wider engagement
Social Identity	The role of continuity in preserving societal identity while embracing change.	Rituals that retain their essence but adopt new forms of expression (e.g., using digital tools in community rituals)

For example, traditional community rituals, such as religious festivals or agricultural celebrations, may continue for generations. However, over time, these practices may incorporate modern elements like digital technology or social media to enhance participation and reach a wider audience. This balance between preserving the core of the tradition and adapting to contemporary circumstances helps societies maintain a sense of continuity while navigating change. Thus, understanding the interplay between tradition and innovation is crucial for comprehending the dynamics of societal evolution.

9.2 Social Adaptation in Times of Rapid Change

Adaptation refers to the capacity of individuals and institutions to respond to social, economic, and environmental challenges. Societies that encourage learning, innovation, and flexibility are better equipped to manage uncertainty.

Social Adaptation in Times of Rapid Change refers to the ability of individuals, communities, and institutions to adjust to new conditions, whether those are economic, technological, environmental, or social challenges. Societies that foster a culture of learning, innovation, and flexibility are more capable of navigating uncertainty and minimizing the negative effects of rapid change.

Adaptation allows societies to evolve in response to challenges. For instance, during economic disruptions or crises (such as a pandemic or natural disaster), communities that embraced digital tools were better equipped to maintain essential functions, such as education, work, and communication. By leveraging technology, they could continue operations, reduce disruptions, and ultimately adapt to the new realities imposed by external challenges.

9.3 Resilience, Community, and Collective Action

Social resilience emerges from strong social networks, shared values, and collective problem-solving. Communities that support cooperation and trust can recover more quickly from crises and transitions.

Resilience, Community, and Collective Action refer to the ability of communities to withstand and recover from crises through solidarity, collaboration, and shared responsibility. Social resilience is strengthened by strong social networks, a sense of shared values, and collective problem-solving mechanisms. When communities are built on cooperation and mutual trust, they can effectively manage adversity and navigate transitions.

Communities with established networks of support-whether informal (such as family and friends) or formal (such as local organizations and self-help groups)-are more likely to bounce back quickly from disruptions like natural disasters, economic downturns, or social unrest. This resilience is rooted in the ability of community members to come together, share resources, and support one another during tough times.

9.4 Envisioning Sustainable Social Futures

The future of social change depends on ethical decision-making, inclusive governance, and sustainable development. Societies must balance technological progress with social responsibility. Reflecting on possible futures encourages proactive planning rather than reactive responses to change.

Envisioning Sustainable Social Futures involves planning for long-term social change that prioritizes ethical decision-making, inclusive governance, and sustainable development. As societies progress technologically, it becomes essential to ensure that this progress is aligned with social responsibility and environmental sustainability. By focusing on sustainable futures, societies can address current challenges while preparing for future opportunities and risks.

Ethical decision-making ensures that technological advances and development projects contribute positively to society without exacerbating inequalities or environmental harm. Inclusive governance promotes participation from all sectors of society, ensuring that all voices are heard and considered in the decision-making process. Sustainable development seeks to meet the needs of the present without compromising the ability of future generations to meet their own needs.

Reflection on Possible Futures : Envisioning potential futures encourages proactive planning rather than simply reacting to challenges as they arise. Societies that engage in this kind of forward-thinking can anticipate and address issues such as climate change, inequality, and technological disruption before they become crises. This approach fosters resilience, adaptability, and long-term well-being.

Aspect	Description	Example
Ethical Decision-Making	Making choices that prioritize fairness, justice, and societal well-being in the face of progress.	Ensuring tech developments, like AI, are used responsibly, with equity and fairness in mind.
Inclusive Governance	Involving all sectors of society in decision-making processes to ensure diverse perspectives.	Community-led decision-making in urban planning or policy reforms.

Sustainable Development	Meeting current needs without compromising the ability of future generations to meet their own.	Transitioning to renewable energy sources to reduce dependency on fossil fuels.
Proactive Planning for the Future	Anticipating challenges and opportunities in order to create long-term solutions.	Cities implementing smart technology for energy efficiency and sustainability, preparing for future needs.

Multiple Choice Questions (MCQs)

1. Which of the following best describes "social adaptation" in times of rapid change?

a) The ability of a society to maintain the status quo
b) The ability to resist all forms of external influence
c) The capacity to adjust to social, economic, and environmental challenges
d) The rejection of modern technology

Answer: c) The capacity to adjust to social, economic, and environmental challenges

2. What is a key factor that contributes to social resilience?

a) Isolation from global developments
b) Strong social networks and collective problem-solving
c) Technological advancement without social considerations
d) Political authority concentration

Answer: b) Strong social networks and collective problem-solving

3. How can communities enhance their ability to recover from crises?

a) By limiting communication between community members
b) By promoting individualism over collective action
c) By fostering cooperation, trust, and community organizations
d) By avoiding external help during a crisis

Answer: c) By fostering cooperation, trust, and community organizations

4. What is the focus of "envisioning sustainable social futures"?

a) Maximizing technological progress without considering social impact
b) Planning for long-term social change that balances technology, ethics, and sustainability
c) Focusing solely on short-term economic growth
d) Rejecting technological advancements in favour of traditional methods

Answer: b) Planning for long-term social change that balances technology, ethics, and sustainability

5. Which of the following is an example of "proactive planning" for future social challenges?

a) Waiting for social issues to arise before addressing them
b) Ignoring future technology and social changes
c) Anticipating future challenges such as climate change and implementing strategies like renewable energy
d) Focusing only on economic growth without considering social consequences

Answer: c) Anticipating future challenges such as climate change and implementing strategies like renewable energy

Short Answer Questions

1. What is meant by social resilience, and why is it important for communities?

2. Explain how inclusive governance contributes to sustainable social futures.
3. How do technological advancements affect social change, and what role does ethical decision-making play?
4. What is the relationship between continuity and change in social systems?
5. How can communities foster adaptation during periods of economic disruption?

Long Answer Questions

1. Discuss the concept of social adaptation. How does it enable communities to navigate challenges and manage transitions effectively? Include examples of communities that have adapted successfully to rapid changes.
2. Analyse the role of community-based organizations in fostering resilience. How do these groups contribute to collective problem-solving and recovery in times of crisis? Provide real-life examples of their impact.
3. Explain how sustainable development is integrated into the vision of a socially resilient future. Discuss the balance between technological progress, social responsibility, and environmental sustainability.
4. In your opinion, how can societies balance the tension between continuity (preserving traditions) and change (embracing innovation) in order to achieve long-term social stability? Provide examples where this balance has been achieved or failed.
5. Evaluate the significance of ethical decision-making in the face of technological advancements. How can societies ensure that technological progress aligns with ethical values, and what are the potential consequences of neglecting this alignment?

References

Chapter 1: Society in Motion – Foundations of Social Change

1. **The Sociological Imagination** – Mills, C. W. (1959). *The Sociological Imagination*. Oxford University Press.
2. **Social Change** – Moore, W. E. (1963). *Social Change*. Prentice-Hall.
3. **Sociology** – Giddens, A. (2017). *Sociology* (8th ed.). Polity Press.

Chapter 2: Culture, Identity, and the Transformation of Social Norms

1. **The Interpretation of Cultures** – Geertz, C. (1973). *The Interpretation of Cultures*. Basic Books.
2. **Identity** – Castells, M. (2010). *The Power of Identity*. Wiley-Blackwell.
3. **Cultural Sociology** – Alexander, J. C. (2003). *The Meanings of Social Life*. Oxford University Press.

Chapter 3: Economic Transitions and the Reshaping of Social Life

1. **The Great Transformation** – Polanyi, K. (1944). *The Great Transformation*. Beacon Press.
2. **Capitalism and Modern Social Theory** – Giddens, A. (1971). *Capitalism and Modern Social Theory*. Cambridge University Press.
3. **The Precariat** – Standing, G. (2011). *The Precariat: The New Dangerous Class*. Bloomsbury.

Chapter 4: Technology, Media, and the Digital Social Order

1. **The Rise of the Network Society** – Castells, M. (2010). *The Rise of the Network Society*. Wiley-Blackwell.
2. **The Shallows** – Carr, N. (2010). *The Shallows*. W. W. Norton.
3. **UNESCO** – UNESCO. (2021). *Global Education Monitoring Report: Technology in Education*.

Chapter 5: Politics, Power, and Social Movements in a Changing World

1. Power – Lukes, S. (1974). *Power: A Radical View*. Macmillan.
2. Social Movements 1768–2004 – Tilly, C. (2004). *Social Movements, 1768–2004*. Paradigm Publishers.
3. Democracy and Its Critics – Dahl, R. A. (1989). *Democracy and Its Critics*. Yale University Press.

Chapter 6: Family, Education, and Social Institutions in Transition

1. The Family – Morgan, D. H. J. (1996). *Family Connections*. Polity Press.
2. Education and Society – Collins, R. (1979). *The Credential Society*. Academic Press.
3. Institutions and Organizations – Scott, W. R. (2013). *Institutions and Organizations*. Sage.

Chapter 7: Globalization, Migration, and Cross-Cultural Interactions

1. Globalization – Giddens, A. (1999). *Runaway World*. Profile Books.
2. International Organization for Migration – IOM. (2022). *World Migration Report*.
3. The Location of Culture – Bhabha, H. K. (1994). *The Location of Culture*. Routledge.

Chapter 8: Inequality, Social Justice, and Emerging Divides

1. The Spirit Level – Wilkinson, R., & Pickett, K. (2009). *The Spirit Level*. Penguin.
2. Capital in the Twenty-First Century – Piketty, T. (2014). *Capital in the Twenty-First Century*. Harvard University Press.
3. Justice – Sandel, M. (2009). *Justice: What's the Right Thing to Do?* Farrar, Straus and Giroux.

Chapter 9: The Future of Social Change – Continuity, Adaptation, and Resilience

1. **Risk Society** – Beck, U. (1992). *Risk Society*. Sage.
2. **Resilience Thinking** – Walker, B., & Salt, D. (2006). *Resilience Thinking*. Island Press.
3. **United Nations** – United Nations. (2015). *Transforming Our World: The 2030 Agenda for Sustainable Development*.

Appendix

1. Glossary of Key Terms

- **Social Change:** Significant alterations in societal structures, values, norms, and behaviours over time. It includes both large-scale transformations (e.g., industrialization) and more subtle shifts in societal values.

- **Globalization:** The process by which businesses, cultures, and societies become interconnected through the exchange of ideas, goods, services, and people across borders.

- **Social Norms:** Unwritten rules and expectations governing social behaviour within a group or society. They evolve over time based on cultural and societal shifts.

- **Cultural Identity:** A person's sense of belonging to a particular culture, shaped by shared values, language, religion, and traditions.

- **Inequality:** Unequal distribution of resources, opportunities, and power among different social groups, often based on factors such as class, race, gender, and education.

- **Social Justice:** The concept of creating a fair and equal society where all individuals have the opportunity to access resources, rights, and privileges.

- **Migration:** The movement of people from one place to another, either within a country or across borders, often due to economic, social, or political factors.

- **Multiculturalism:** The coexistence of diverse cultural groups within a society, often celebrated as a form of diversity and inclusion.

- **Resilience:** The ability of individuals or societies to recover, adapt, and thrive despite challenges or disruptions, including economic crises, natural disasters, or social upheaval.
- **Digital Divide:** The gap between individuals or communities who have access to modern information technology and those who do not, often due to socioeconomic factors.

2. Data Sources and Datasets

- **World Bank Open Data:** Comprehensive and globally recognized datasets related to economic, social, and environmental indicators. It offers insights into global development trends.
  https://data.worldbank.org/
- **United Nations Data:** A wide range of datasets covering demographic, social, economic, and environmental data collected by UN agencies, useful for understanding global trends and inequalities.
  https://data.un.org/
- **OECD Economic Outlook:** A valuable source of data on global economic performance, providing reports on national economies, inequality, and social policies.
  https://www.oecd.org/economic-outlook/
- **Pew Research Centre:** Datasets and reports on social trends, public opinion, and demographics, especially focusing on globalization, technology, and political movements.
  https://www.pewresearch.org/
- **International Migration Report (IOM):** A key source for global migration data, capturing trends and policy impacts on migration patterns.
  https://www.iom.int/world-migration-report

3. Tools and Frameworks

- **SPSS (Statistical Package for the Social Sciences):** A widely used software tool for conducting statistical analysis in social science research, useful for analysing surveys and demographic data.
- **NVivo:** A qualitative data analysis software that assists researchers in organizing, analysing, and visualizing data from interviews, focus groups, and ethnographies.
- **STATA:** A powerful data analysis tool used in economics, sociology, and other social sciences for managing and analysing data, especially with complex datasets.
- **Gephi:** An open-source network analysis tool used for mapping and visualizing social networks, which can be valuable for studying migration, communication flows, and other complex social phenomena.
- **R Programming:** A statistical computing environment used for data manipulation, analysis, and visualization, particularly useful for analysing large and complex datasets in sociology and social sciences.

4. References for Further Reading

- **Bauman, Z. (2000).** *Liquid Modernity*. Polity Press.
  A crucial text exploring the fluidity and transformation of social structures in the modern world, examining the impact of globalization and technological change on society.
- **Giddens, A. (1990).** *The Consequences of Modernity*. Stanford University Press.
  Giddens' seminal work on the dynamics of modernity, focusing on how industrialization, globalization, and rapid technological change shape societies.

- **Sennett, R. (1998).** *The Corrosion of Character: The Personal Consequences of Work in the New Capitalism.* W. W. Norton & Company. An insightful exploration of how economic and social changes affect individual identity and the social fabric of communities.
- **Harvey, D. (2005).** *A Brief History of Neoliberalism.* Oxford University Press.
  Harvey's analysis of neoliberal economic policies and their global impact, exploring the restructuring of economies and the rise of inequality.
- **Castells, M. (2010).** *The Rise of the Network Society.* Wiley-Blackwell. A foundational text on how the information age and technological networks are reshaping global economies, politics, and social structures.

5. Future Directions in Social Change Research

- **The Role of Artificial Intelligence in Social Movements:** As AI continues to evolve, its impact on organizing, communication, and mobilization for social justice movements will be a critical area of study. Exploring the ethical implications of AI in decision-making processes, surveillance, and privacy will become increasingly important.
- **Climate Change and Social Justice:** With the growing threat of climate change, future research will need to address the social consequences of environmental degradation. Understanding how marginalized communities are disproportionately affected will be crucial for promoting equitable environmental policies.
- **The Digitalization of Education and its Impact on Inequality:** The future of education, particularly in developing nations, will be shaped by the increasing availability of online learning platforms. However, the digital divide poses a significant challenge, and future research will need to focus on how to bridge this gap.

- **Global Health and Inequality:** The COVID-19 pandemic highlighted global health disparities and the links between health, economy, and social stability. Future research must focus on how global health systems can be reformed to provide equitable healthcare for all.
- **Social Networks and Identity in the Digital Age:** With the rise of social media platforms and digital spaces for interaction, the future of socialization, identity formation, and group dynamics will be heavily influenced by digital environments. Research should explore how these networks shape personal identities and societal interactions.

6. Summary of Key Points

- **Social Change is Inevitable:** Societies are continually evolving in response to technological, cultural, economic, and political forces. The changes may be slow or abrupt, but they are a constant feature of human existence.
    - **Technology and Media are Key Drivers:** Technology and media have a transformative effect on how societies function, impacting everything from the economy to personal relationships. The digital age has especially brought about rapid change in communication, access to information, and social organization.
- **Globalization and Migration are Reshaping Social Norms:** Increasing globalization and migration have led to greater cultural exchange and diversity, but have also raised challenges related to identity, inequality, and integration. These shifts require new frameworks for understanding social cohesion.

ABOUT THE AUTHOR

Dr. Sanat Kumar Singha (b. 07 January 1984) is an accomplished sociologist and educator, currently serving as Assistant Professor of Sociology at Raiganj Surendranath Mahavidyalaya, Uttar Dinajpur, West Bengal. He completed his B.A. (Honours) in Sociology from the University of North Bengal in 2005 and his M.A. in Sociology from the University of Burdwan in 2007, and qualified the West Bengal State Eligibility Test (SET) in 2009. He began his academic career as a part-time lecturer at Gour Mahavidyalaya, Malda, where he taught from 2008 to 2016 before joining Raiganj Surendranath Mahavidyalaya in December 2016.

Beyond teaching, Dr. Singha actively contributes to institutional development as Programme Officer of NSS Unit-I and as a member of the Career Counselling Committee. His research interests include women empowerment, self-help groups, migration, social media, and contemporary social issues. He has authored and co-authored several scholarly publications and presented papers at national and international forums. In 2025, he was awarded a Ph.D. in Sociology from Maharaja Agrasen Himalayan Garhwal University, further strengthening his profile as a dedicated scholar and socially engaged academic.

10. E-LIBRAIRIE – France (French online bookstore)
11. Everand – India (Everand Book Distributor is based in India)
12. EXLIBRIS – Switzerland
13. Fable – United Kingdom (UK/Europe digital subscription book service)
14. Flipkart – India
15. GANDHI.com – Mexico (Librerías Gandhi)
16. Google Book – United States (Google LLC)
17. Google Audio Book – United States (Google LLC)
18. IBS.IT – Italy Wikipedia
19. Indigo – Canada
20. Kobo – Canada Wikipedia
21. Kindle – United States (Amazon product)
22. LAFELTRINELLI – Italy Wikipedia
23. Lehmanns – Germany
24. Lulu – United States
25. MORAWA – Austria
26. Rakuten Japan – Japan (Rakuten)
27. Smashwords – United States
28. Tolino / Thalia – Germany (Tolino is a German-language eBook ecosystem, Thalia DE)

29. Vivlio – France

30. Saxo – Denmark (Saxo.com)

31. YES24 – South Korea

and others.

🎁 You will receive 20 physical author copies FREE to your Indian address.

⭐ You can also receive 5 book reviews:

* 3 reviews by eminent university professors

* 2 reviews from your own group/colleagues/seniors/teachers

www.books.wissira.us

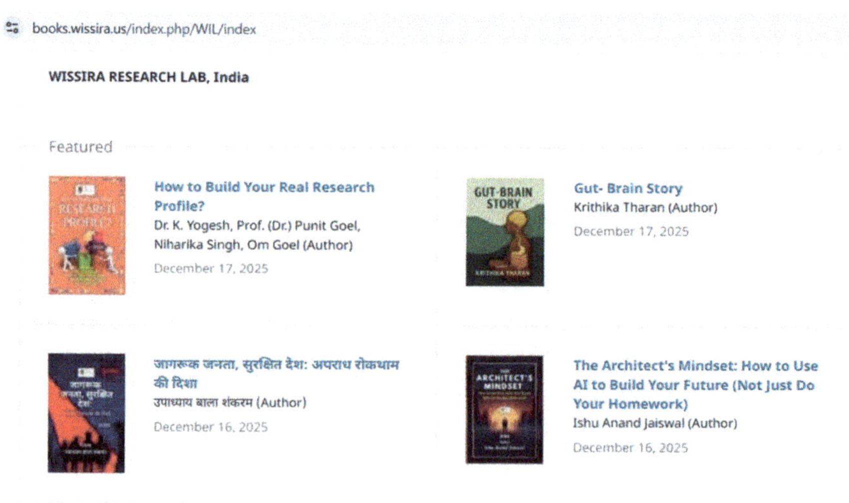

www.books.wissira.us

DOI: https://doi.org/10.63345/book.wrl.2512000324

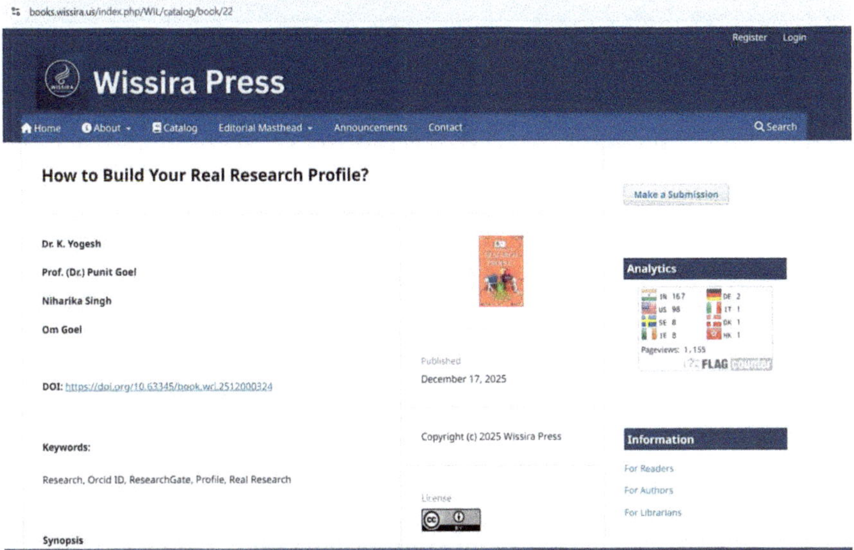

https://books.wissira.us/index.php/WIL/login

https://books.wissira.us/index.php/WIL/catalog

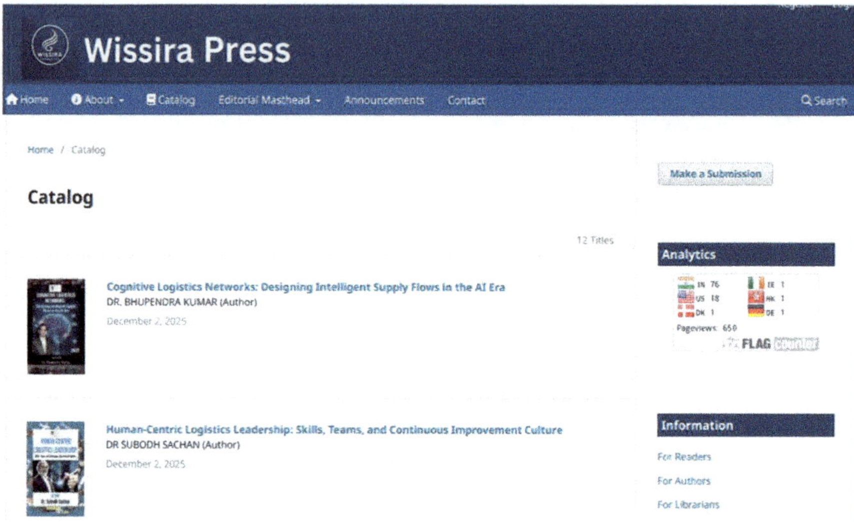

https://books.wissira.us/index.php/WIL/about/contact

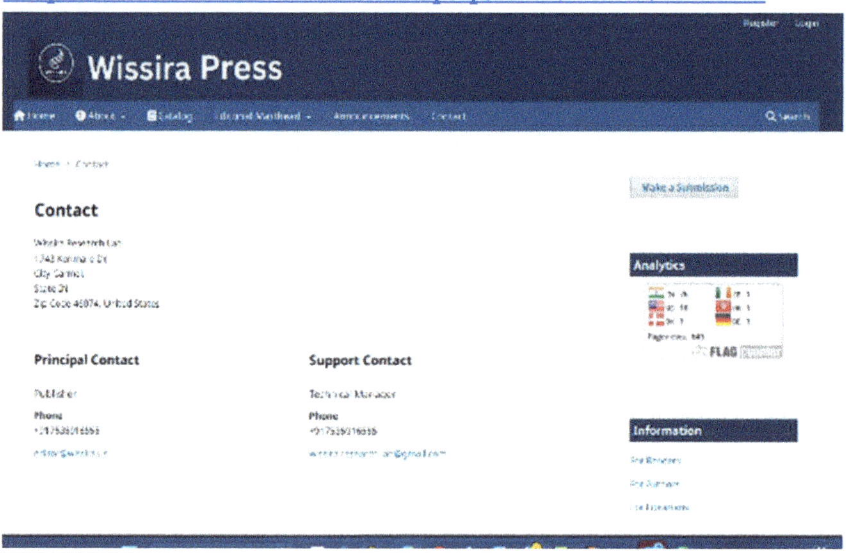

https://www.amazon.in/dp/B0G7MQFD2L

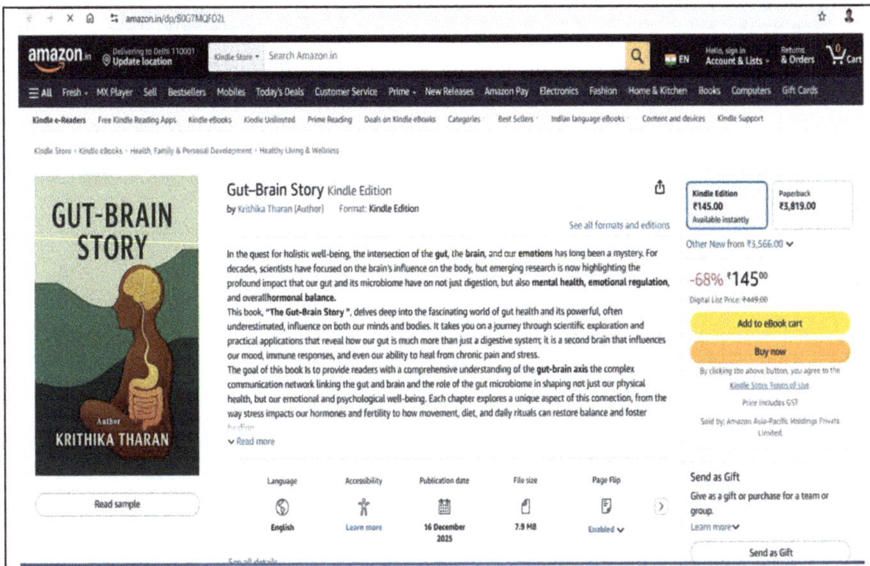

https://books.apple.com/us/book/the-architects-mindset-how-to-use-ai-to-build-your/id6756545876

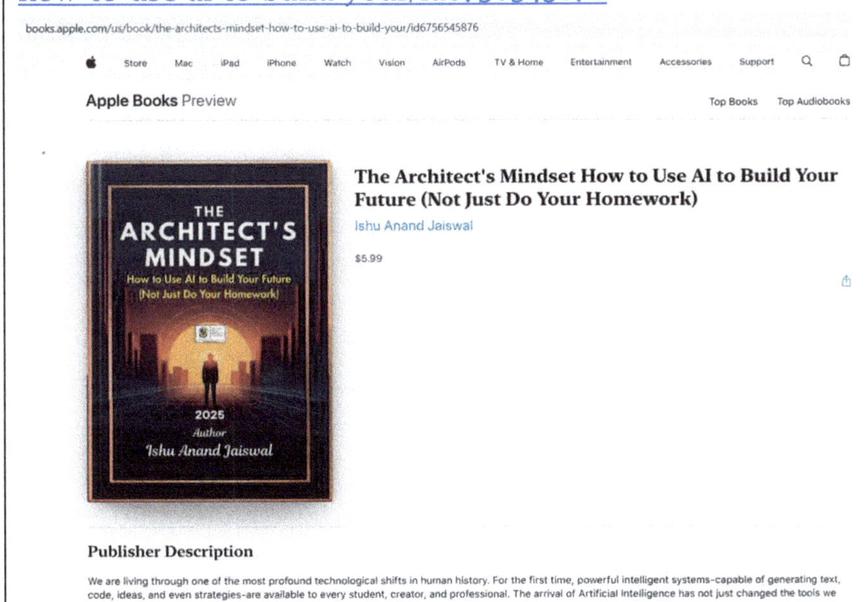

Flipkart:
https://tinyurl.com/WissieaPressBook250306Human

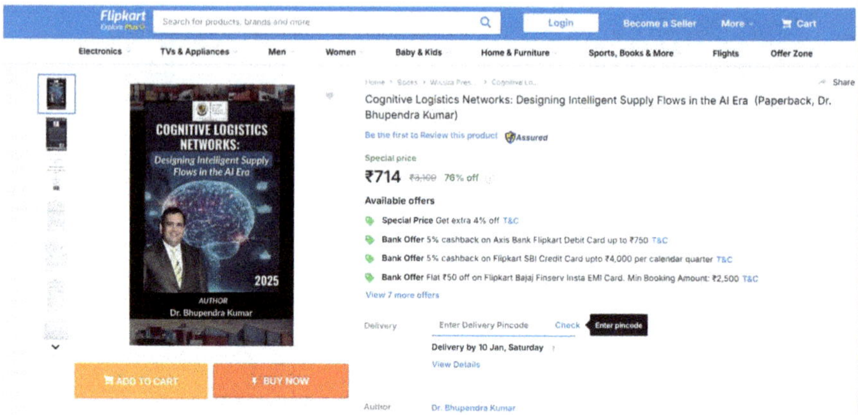

https://play.google.com/store/audiobooks/details?id=AQAAAEAa9DeoPM

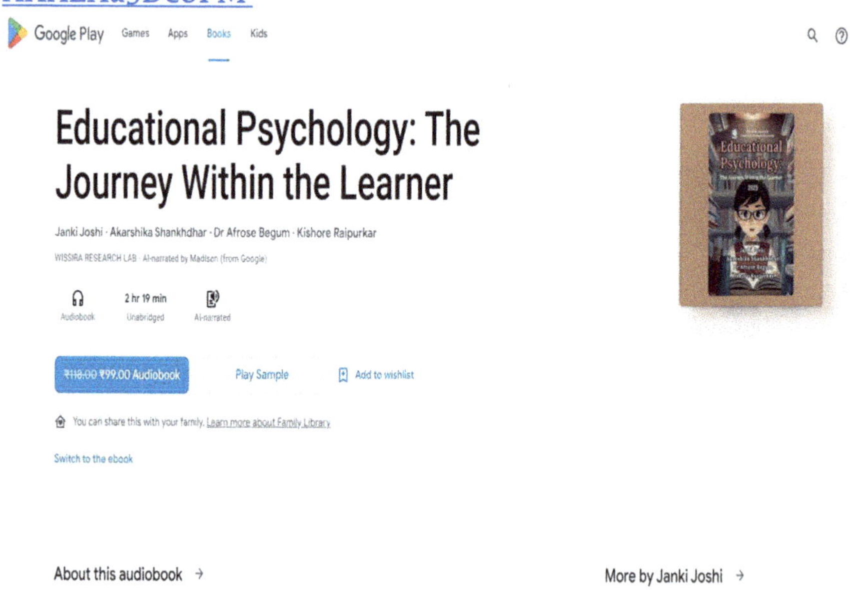

https://shop.vivlio.com/product/9798232547615_9798232547615_10020/human-centric-logistics-leadership-skills-teams-and-continuous-improvement-culture

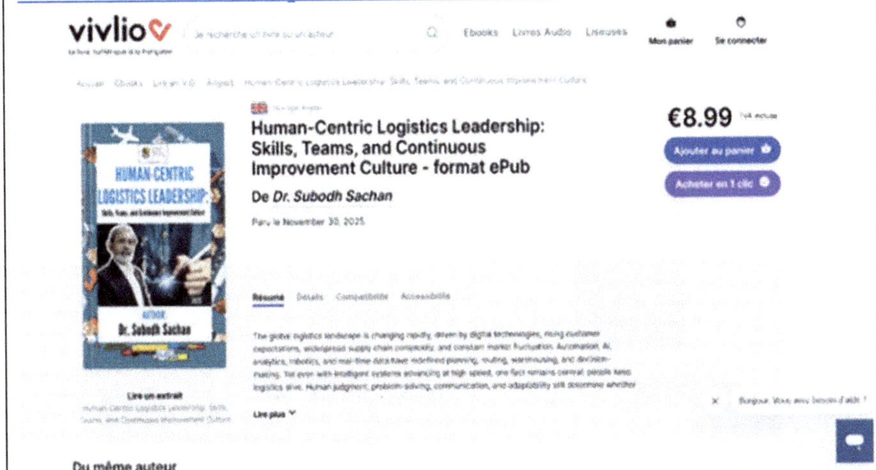

https://www.kobo.com/in/en/ebook/from-shakespeare-to-tagore-reinterpreting-english-literature-through-indian-sensibility?sId=070486d4-8aef-4220-a1d2-26bb2ba8ecb6&ssId=3FJLsnB4eTMdnS31kaTcM

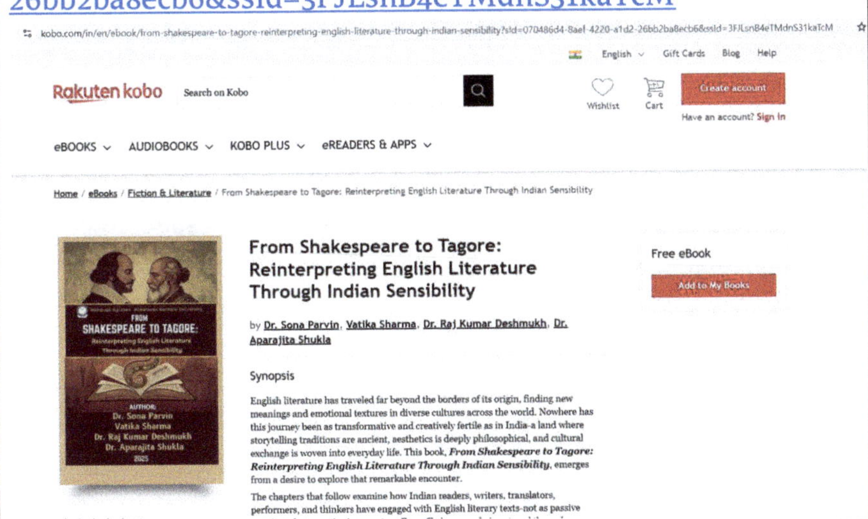

https://fable.co/book/x-9798230804772

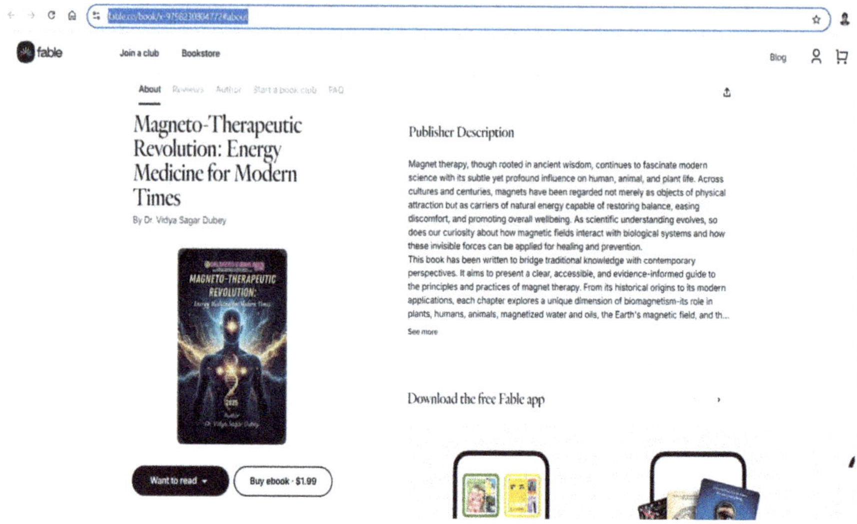

https://www.lulu.com/shop/dr-subodh-sachan/human-centric-logistics-leadership/ebook/product-rmj4erq.html?q=Human-Centric+Logistics+Leadership%3A+Skills%2C+Teams%2C+and+Continuous+Improvement+Culture&page=1&pageSize=

4

https://play.google.com/store/audiobooks/details?id=AQAAAEDqoRHh6M

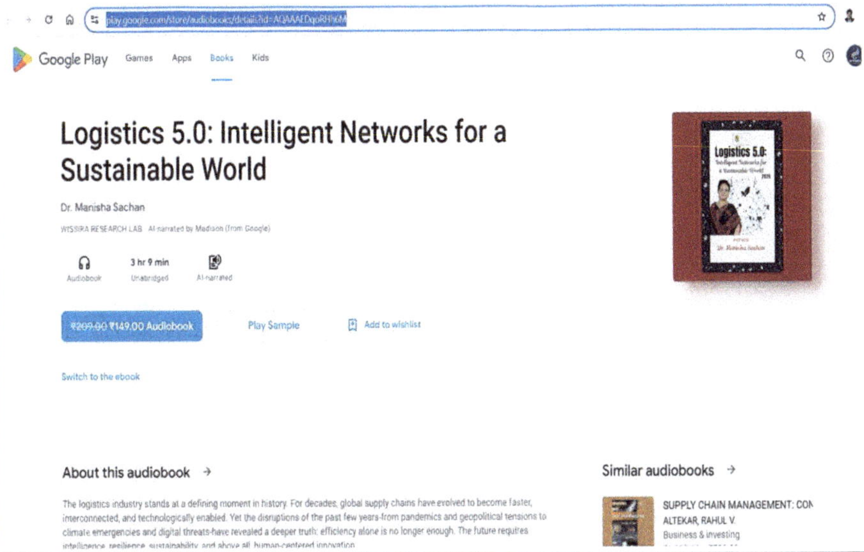

https://play.google.com/store/books/details?id=TbmfEQAAQBAJ

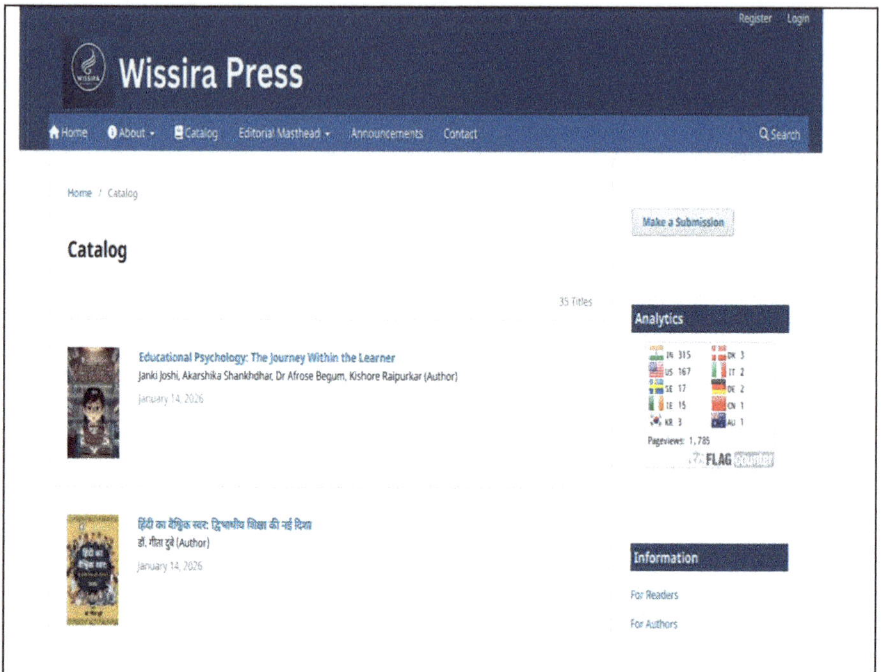

https://www.smashwords.com/books/view/1943936

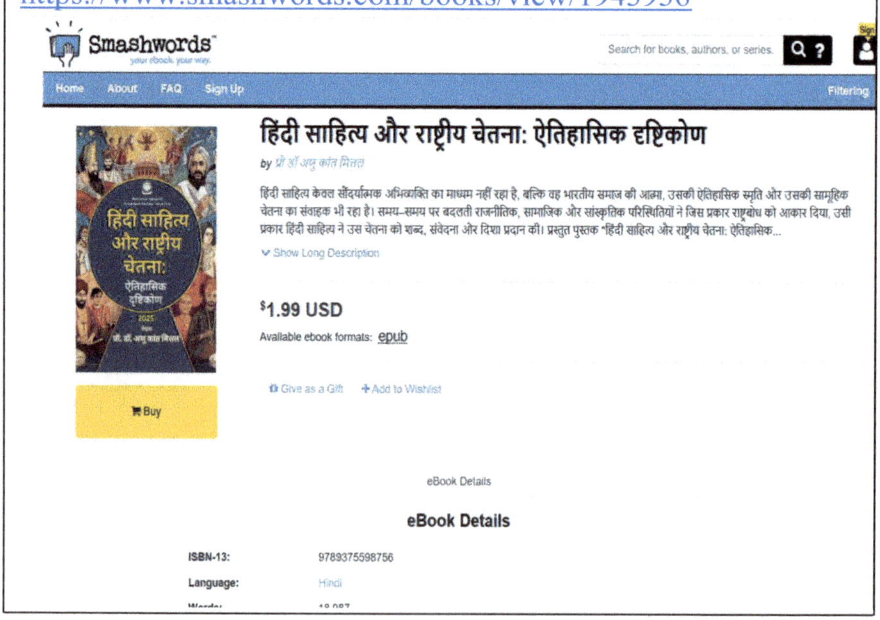

Amazon Kindle

Amazon

Flipkart

LULU

Apple Books

Barnes & Nobles

Everand

Fable

Kobo

Analytics

IN	135	IT	1
US	84	DK	1
SE	8	HK	1
IE	8	DE	1

Pageviews: 1,012

FLAG counter

Information

For Readers

For Authors

For Librarians

Keywords

sustain long-term operational excellence.

Across the nine chapters of this work, readers will find a structured and practical approach to understanding how leadership influences logistics outcomes. Beginning with the foundations of human-centric leadership, the book explores essential competencies such as communication, empathy, decision-making, and ethical responsibility-skills that enable leaders to build credibility and trust in high-pressure environments. It then moves deeper into the dynamics of teamwork, motivation, and empowerment, highlighting how resilient and collaborative teams become the backbone of

Smashwords

Tolino

Vivlio

Google Books

---

www.ingramcontent.com/pod-product-compliance
Ingram Content Group UK Ltd.
Pitfield, Milton Keynes, MK11 3LW, UK
UKHW021411190726
13845UKWH00028B/1015

9 789375 594802